Off Track Planet's
TRAVEL GUIDE
for the
YOUNG, SEXY, AND BROKE

BY THE EDITORS OF OTP

FREDDIE PIKOVSKY *and* ANNA STAROSTINETSKAYA

RUNNING PRESS
PHILADELPHIA

© 2017 by Off Track Planet
Published by Running Press,
An Imprint of Perseus Books, LLC.,
A Subsidiary of Hachette Book Group, Inc.
All rights reserved under the Pan-American and International Copyright Conventions

Printed in China

Books published by Running Press are available at special discounts for bulk purchases in the United States
by corporations, institutions, and other organizations. For more information, please contact
the Special Markets Department at Perseus Books, 2300 Chestnut Street, Suite 200,
Philadelphia, PA 19103, or call (800) 810-4145, ext. 5000, or e-mail special.markets@perseusbooks.com.

ISBN 978-0-7624-5925-4
Library of Congress Control Number: 2016939294

E-book ISBN 978-0-7624-6118-9

9   8   7   6   5   4   3   2   1
Digit on the right indicates the number of this printing

Cover design by Susan Van Horn
Interior design by Corinda Cook
Edited by Jessica Fromm
Typography: Neutraface, Archer, Bebas, Korolev, Roboto, Prohibition, and Wisdom Script

Running Press Book Publishers
2300 Chestnut Street
Philadelphia, PA 19103-4371

Visit us on the web!
www.runningpress.com

CONTENTS

INTRODUCTION

In the summer of 2009, a passionate group of young travelers met in a Brooklyn hostel and were soon bound together by a common vision: changing the world means seeing it. Off Track Planet was born from this vision, and through our website (Off trackplanet.com) we began communicating the appeal of travel to our ADD-ridden, social media- and smartphone-addicted peers with the hope of inspiring them to give back to the world by exploring it.

We set out to create movement in the world by showing Americans the value of travel beyond just "taking a vacation." We believe that luxury travel is for people with arthritis; backpacking, with an open mind and empty bank account, is the best way to learn about the world.

If thinking about traveling automatically triggers an excuse that's keeping you grounded, let's get a few things straight right away.

MONEY

"I CAN'T AFFORD IT."

We've all seen the bottom of a Cup-O-Noodle more than once. So how can you afford to travel? By redefining travel to be more about hostels and street food and less about resorts and cruises, the biggest initial expense then comes down to that first flight out of the country. Some destinations may be out of your budget, but there's no reason why you can't afford getting down to Central America when you can find flights for under $600 round trip. Even parts of Europe are relatively affordable to fly into at times. And once you're abroad,

holy shit do you have affordable options. You can learn everything about tango in Buenos Aires, catch some good karma at the Chao Phraya temples in Bangkok, and get crispy brown at clothing-optional Greek beaches—all for free if you just get your ass over there.

SAFETY

"I'M SCARED OF GETTING SHANKED ABROAD."

Kidnappings, murders, rapes, and robberies happen everywhere, all the time. The truth is, America's violent crime rate is higher than that of many industrialized countries all over the world. Places like Ireland, Germany, the Netherlands, Canada, and Norway have incredibly low stats when it comes to crime. Sure, if you go to war-torn territories in the Middle East or stand around aimlessly in the border towns of Mexico, shit will go down. Cure your fear with knowledge (e.g., the book you're holding in your hands) and simple common sense.

HEALTH

"I'LL CATCH SOME DEADLY FOREIGN DISEASE."

Realistically, your biggest travel health concern is diarrhea, and you can have a fatal case of the shits. But c'mon, diarrhea is something we've all had some experience with. The true fear here lies in the crap our media drills into our heads about foreign germs and bird viruses. If you get the flu, break your arm, or just feel plain shitty, every country has a hospital, clinic, or pharmacy that will take care of you.

HOSTELS

"HOSTELS SCARE THE SHIT OUT OF ME."

Hostels sound like a bunch of dirty, disease-spreading halfway houses, inhabited by crackheads and creeps, right? Despite what you've seen in the movies, hostels are generally safe and fun budget accommodations that allow you to meet like-minded travelers. You can exchange travel stories, cook meals, and, if you get sneaky, have the sexytime. Still not sold? Options like Couchsurfing or nailing down a decent Airbnb abroad will also get you into a bed for cheap.

LANGUAGE BARRIER

"NO ONE WILL UNDERSTAND THE WORDS THAT ARE COMING OUT OF MY MOUTH."

We all had to learn to speak at some point. Before then? Well, there were a lot of hand gestures and noises to get our points across. You can resort to your baby body language in foreign territory and get by fine. Additionally, a good portion of the world will probably understand you, even if you're speaking only English. You can also tutor local college students in English and barter for help with their native language or take a few formal courses while you're there.

TIME WASTED

"I DON'T HAVE THE TIME."

Your parents may think that traveling is a huge waste of time, all about getting drunk and partying (and some of it should be), but it has real value that your lame day-to-day routine at home just can't match. Add up your morning commute, time on Facebook, and those days you're just too bored with life to get out of bed. What's that equal? A whole bunch of empty time. Every minute of travel is an opportunity to learn something new. You can really milk the value of travel—and add value to your résumé and college applications—by volunteering or studying abroad.

This book isn't organized like a traditional travel guide, and we don't spoon-feed you information on any one destination. Instead, we've split the book up into three parts. The first is a collection of oddities, traditions, fascinating events, and happenings in various destinations around the world, divided up by interests. The second section is all about the practical logistics of travel and will help you get your shit ready for takeoff. The last section is a sampling of the work, study, and volunteer opportunities available abroad to help you continue traveling with purpose once you're hooked.

Sure, you could convince yourself of a million reasons why you'd love to travel but just can't swing it right now. But what would you do if you weren't afraid? Get a backpack, book a flight, order a drink, and stop making excuses.

PART 1

GET OUT THERE

Reignite your sense of adventure by conquering the world's greatest mountains, oceans, and footpaths. Let your artistic eye wander and find something visually stimulating in the streets and alleyways of even the most remote places. Gather unique pieces and fashionable inspiration from around the world to create an eclectic wardrobe that no stateside copycat can duplicate. Let your passion for food drive you to the culinary greatness found only in Paris or the uncommon foods people concoct into edibles in Southeast Asia. Pack a guitar or buy a banjo; join a beachy drum circle or hit up a live show; scream your lungs out and stir your soul to the vast array of sounds being pumped through the world's bars, venues, and festivals. Party like it's your job and hook up with locals from here to Timbuktu. No matter what you're interested in, there are enough options out there to feed your desire for just about anything.

ADVENTURE AND EXTREME SPORTS

The landscape of the world, with its soaring peaks, drop cliffs, tropical jungles, array of underwater animal life, and bumpy overland terrain is meant to be taken head-on and not just viewed from a fancy hotel balcony. Feed your inner adrenaline junkie some quality adventure by tossing yourself into the canyons of Interlaken, carving your way through Canada's powdery terrain, and slapping on a wetsuit to explore Australia's Great Barrier Reef. Leave no stone unturned, no mountain unscaled, and unlock the next level of thrill by expanding your adventures worldwide. Everyone knows that adrenaline pumps hardest in unfamiliar territory.

REEFER MADNESS

The largest structure on the planet made up entirely of living organisms, the Great Barrier Reef (GBR) is a live seafood soup filled with crazy-looking and endangered animals swimming at you from all angles. A UNESCO World Heritage site, this reef is home to 1,500 species of fish. Throw some scuba gear on your mammalian ass and discover what makes this reef so great.

SCUBA

The GBR stretches 1,600 miles along the Queensland coast in the Coral Sea, and the best way to experience it is to submerge yourself deep into its crevices. Eighty-pound grouper cruise by, schools of barracuda eye you cautiously, reef shark silhouettes loom in the distance, sea turtles float by, drunk on life, and Nemo feverishly defends his nest all around a reef of hard and soft coral that no box of Crayola could ever color-code. There are countless ways to see these billions of coral polyps. Here's a short list to get you bright-eyed:

Cairns

The scuba capital of Australia has no shortage of tour agencies to get you to the reef. Shop around to avoid rip-offs or book at a well-reviewed hostel. The GBR is a long boat ride from Cairns, so an overnight trip is the best way to see it. You can get two days with three dives each (including a night dive) with food and lodging on a live-aboard boat for about $560. Some of these bigger boats feel like touristy assembly lines; make sure to check boat reviews online before paying.

SS Yongola Wreck Dive

One hundred years ago, the *SS Yongola* passenger ship disappeared in a cyclone, along with all 122 people on board. This football field–size mass grave quickly became a cushy new underwater neighborhood, gentrified by the swankiest of fish. Local dive shops claim you see more species of fish on this one wreck dive than you do in ten dives anywhere else on the reef.

Shark-Feeding Dive

If you do a weeklong live-aboard jaunt out to the Osprey Reef, you'll see the best collections of the reef's sharks, especially when the dive ops run a shark-feeding dive at North Horn. Dozens of gray sharks, silvertips, and sometimes hammerheads and tiger sharks circle overhead and bolt past you for giant chunks of the provided fish carcasses. Try not to crap your wetsuit.

Too Legit, Too Legit to Quit

While it's not as cheap as Asia or Central America, you can get certified to dive anywhere along the reef. (Cairns cranks out more certifications than anywhere else in the world.) As a bonus, your four certification dives are actually at the GBR (as opposed to in some Midwest rock quarry). Snorkeling is a decent consolation if you can't dive, but it'll feel like a threesome gone wrong as you look longingly at the reef rather than being a part of it.

SKYDIVING

The GBR is visible from space. Don't take our word for it—head up that way and see for yourself. Instead of squinting through a tiny airplane window, jump out of that bad boy for a better view. As wind relentlessly pummels your face and howls past your ears, you'll hit terminal velocity in a sixty-second free fall that'll seem like a lifetime. Once you're jolted to a stop with the release of your chute, you'll feel suspended in midair, soaking up the views of this world wonder.

The Great Barrier Reef is almost the size of Texas, but climate change is wiping it out faster than Windex wipes schmutz off a windshield. Already called the "So-So Barrier Reef," the GBR is definitely dying. Get there before it's gone.

PACK YOUR MACHETE, THINGS ARE ABOUT TO GET WILD

Covering 2.3 million square miles across nine countries, the Amazon is a portal to a mysteriously green world unlike anything you've ever imagined. Here you can learn how to suck drinking water from vines and how to tell the difference between tree bark that kills and bark that's rumored to cure cancer. You'll cook over an open fire, spice up lunch with coconut-flavored grubs, and wash it down with mint-flavored ants.

THE SPREAD

The vast majority of the jungle is in Brazil, but digging through greenery there is fannypack-heavy and consequently more expensive. Cheaper and farther off the gringo trail, the Bolivian Amazon is concentrated in the northeast of the country.

There are forty-six indigenous tribes in and around the 7,320-square-mile Madidi National Park—most of which is closed off to tourism. To get there, hop on a flight from La Paz to the small airport in Rurrenabaque, or risk a twenty-four-hour bus ride on the world's most dangerous road.

WE DARE YOU NOT TO DIE: BOLIVIA'S DEATH ROAD

Flying down the side of an 11,800-foot mountain—the world's most dangerous road, the Highway of Death or *Camino de la Muerte*—is part sightseeing, part adventure, part death wish, and all completely badass. Hop on a bike and try your hand at staying alive.

The road starts at an icy Andean summit and skids to a halt in the steamy Amazonian Yungas. The gravel will kick you in the face as you narrowly grab hairpin curves. The handlebars will shake, but tell fear to fuck itself. You'll whiz past grazing llamas, jaw-dropping cliff sides, and a drug checkpoint. Better settle for a Huari beer on the bus back to La Paz, but you'll have earned it. Barreling down a mountain at sixty miles per hour is as sweaty and exhilarating as it sounds.

For just over $100, agencies in La Paz can hook you up with wheels, gear, a guide, and perks like free lunch and a postride swim. When you're choosing an agency, remember that the cheaper the tour, the cheaper your equipment, and the bigger your balls must be to make up for it. Over the years, about twenty cyclists never got to the swim. But thousands more have given risk the middle finger and now sport a "I'm a Death Road Survivor" T-shirt as a symbol of their rite of passage. With a little panache and good form, you can easily kick this road to the curb—and live to tell the story.

JUNGLE BOOKING

Rurrenabaque is a little like the American Wild West, a tiny dusty town without an ATM where locals wear a jaguar tooth as a badge of pride. It's also where intrepid travelers hook up with true jungle men to go in deep. With a plethora of the most dangerous animals on Earth and unforgiving terrain, it's almost sure death—not to mention illegal—to go exploring alone. You can book a trip through one of the many agencies that line the streets of Rurrenabaque. Most offer packages that include sit-down meals and a hammock at one of the several ecolodges in Madidi. Lush mountains and rolling banana plantations surround the park, and you'll get there by a two-hour boat ride from town.

HACKING IT ALONE

If you're looking to head out with just a guide and the pack on your back, some agencies offer more rugged trips. A couple offer full-on survival courses where you brave your journey with nothing but a machete and iodine tablets.

You will learn how to feed yourself in the wild, sleep with one eye open, and stand your ground in jungle confrontations (since most anacondas aren't familiar with dismissive phrases like "fuck off"). It's important to figure out what type of experience you want to have and ask as many questions as it takes to find the right guide or tour company.

If you want to bushwhack your way through the muddy brush, pick up a machete at one of the many hardware stores in town. And the bugs are brutal—stock up on DEET to keep the bites at bay.

FIVE ANIMALS YOU'VE NEVER HEARD OF

The Amazon is like a mystery grab bag of life, and when you reach in, sometimes you pull out a regular old toucan and other times, a fistful of fish with wings, floppy-eyed frogs, and plants with feelings (if you are lucky enough to keep your hand while fiddling around in the Amazon bag that is). Here are just a few animals that live in the world's most cryptic jungle:

1. Emperor Tamarin—This guy would be tough competition come Mo-vember.

3. Hoatzin—People call him the "stinkbird" because he smells like manure. As backpackers, we fully understand. We'd probably share a hostel dorm with him, go out for drinks a few times, and make him drunken pasta in the hostel kitchen before noticing any odor irregularities.

4. Skydiving Ant—While ants can do all kinds of crazy things (kill you, for one), this species decided to up the ante by developing the ability to skydive using its ass for counterbalance. Now if it could film itself doing tandem jumps with ants too scared to take the plunge alone, we'd be pretty impressed.

5. T-Rex Leech—The dinosaur of blood-suckers, this leech is very well endowed when it comes to teeth and unfortunately, very poorly endowed when it comes to the parts that matter.

2. Wood-Eating Catfish—He may have been out of the office when all the other catfish got the "you're not a beaver" memo.

WATER SPORT BUFFET

Dipping into various water sports at one beachy destination is fun because you get to see the place from various perspectives while riding an adrenaline high, all without breaking a sweat. Many of the world's beaches offer an array of water sports but charge a high price to play. A quick one-hour flight from Manila, Boracay has all the right moves to tempt you into permanent island residency—for prices that won't get your Speedo in a knot.

GET YOUR WINGS

Using wind-power, kiteboarding (sometimes called kitesurfing) requires a specialty board and a big-ass kite that the rider controls to glide across the surface of the water. Like a multiadventure sport orgy between surfing, paragliding, wakeboarding, windsurfing, and snowboarding, kiteboarding is piss-in-your pants fun and Bulabog Beach is one of the best places in Asia to do it.

Bulabog Beach draws top boarders from all over the world to test their skills over foreign waters. Peak kiteboarding season is November–April, when the off-shore winds blow just right and the primo boarding spot is a small lagoon protected from waves by a coral reef. Glassy water conditions make this a perfect spot for beginners looking to pop their kite boarding cherries, or pros who want to practice backflips on wave-free waters. If all you can manage here is a sloppy belly flop, at least you can gaze at the insane aquatic scenery while the sting wears off.

AMPHIBIOUS PURSUITS

If surfing the seas with the wind as your motor sounds like a kitemare, Boracay has plenty of other adventures under her salt-water-soaked skirt. Complete with coral reefs, canyons, and caves, scuba divers go googly eyed exploring the island from the underside. Hop on a jet ski, graze the water on a skimboard, or play the part of a pretentious speedboat asshole. However you feel like stirring up the ocean, you can do it here relatively cheaply and easily.

SAIL PAST THE CROWDS

It's not in tribute to some surrendered battle or a pale-faced explorer; White Beach simply has white sand. Tons of it. Since people love that pillowy stuff, the beach is littered with bodies during the summer. Sift through the skimpy pickings or hop on a *paraw* (Filipino sailboat) to drift away from the swarm. Bargaining your paraw price with a Filipino sailor won't require learning Tagalog, since most locals speak English. There are usually snorkels on board and your captain will sail you around even more remote beaches to really ditch the crowds —and possibly your bathing suit.

GUANO GO TO THE BAT CAVE?

If crawling in a dark, slippery, dangerous cave filled with bat shit and sea snakes sounds like your idea of a good time, put on some hiking boots (not sandals), buy a flashlight, and head to the northeast of the island, inland from the remote Ilig-Iligan Beach. Hiring a guide (or befriending a Filipino) who knows how to navigate the steep entrance is a good idea. Negotiate a price beforehand to avoid getting ripped off in the dark. Ready to get bat-shit crazy?

Flying Foxes

It's a short hike through a dense forest to the mouth of the cave and the bat-action begins even before you reach the entrance. Be on the lookout for the largest bat in the world, the flying fox bat (a.k.a. fruit bat). No need to fear these cute, cuddly, endangered creatures—they only eat fruit and nectar, not people or eyeballs. The name "flying fox" refers to the mammal's big eyes, furry face, and small ears (like a batty Furby).

To the Bat Cave!

The descent into the cave is steep and slippery with nothing to hold on to but big boulders covered in hot slime. Wear shoes with good traction (and gloves if you have them), to reduce the chances of falling to your death. Also, you will be descending in the dark, so a flashlight is necessary (especially to spot the poisonous sea snakes). Inside the cave, it's deathly hot, hard to breathe, and smells like pure anus–this is normal. The cave is covered in bat shit (guano) from the small, insect-eating bats that live at the bottom. Look up to see the stalactites on the ceiling and down to see the pool of water at the bottom of the cave.

EXTREME UNLIMITED

Bum a cup of kickass from our North American neighbor. Knock on Vancouver's door on your way to Whistler Blackcomb, a monstrous snow resort that you can carve up until your lungs turn purple. Head down the street to Banff and load your ear canals with white water. And finally, get gluttonous in Quebec, the birthplace of the inevitable Canadian food coma, better known as "poutine." This continental colossus offers adventure from every angle, with both winter and summer adrenaline-loaded adventures, just waiting to be manhandled.

WHISTLE WHILE YOU CARVE: SNOWBOARDING VANCOUVER

The holy behemoth of North American mountains, Whistler Blackcomb of British Columbia is often regarded as the greatest snow resort in the world, and is the place to put your shred sled to the test. Clip in your boots and carve a deep trail down these twin mondo mountains.

Coming Down the Mountains

With over 8,000 combined acres of boardable trails, the Whistler and Blackcomb mountains ensure that even the most serious of you snowbums will be happily bombing down the slopes all season long.

Dozens of lifts lead to the 200-plus trails of fresh Vancouver snow canvases that await your craftsmanship. Carve your tightest S's and master your jump turns down Blackcomb's world-rated "Couloir Extreme"—a fifty-two-degree test of how much hell you're willing to put your thighs through. Get tricky on the mountain's Olympic-size superpipe, or head over to Whistler and race through the "Peak-to-Creek" perimeter tour trail of over four miles! Can't decide which mountain you want to tear up today? Get on the "Peak 2 Peak" gondola—a record-breaking scenic ride of a lifetime that connects Blackcomb and Whistler.

UNCHILL YOUR NIPS WITH POUTINE

Soften up your shirt-piercing nips with Canada's trifecta of fat. Quite possibly Quebec's greatest contribution to the planet, poutine is a big ol' ball of cholesterol that can kill lesser men ill-prepared for its addicting glory. With globs of fatty juices and dripping in sticky goo, somewhere beneath its artery-clogging exterior is a Canadian treat that warms you to the core.

Pou-natmony

It consists of three ingredients, piled on top of one another: (1) French fries, (2) gravy, and (3) cheese curds. The fries are piping hot, golden, and somehow still crispy despite the gravy that covers them. The gravy is as thick and sweet as jelly. And the curds? Little nuggets of smooth dairy deliciousness melt into the pile and make little squeaky sounds with every bite. Just reading the ingredients will make you fatter, and it is truly a wonder how Canada's morbid obesity rates are so low. What's more, poutine is normally just a side dish to a main meal! You can essentially get the stuff anywhere across the country, short of Indian restaurants, from 8:00 a.m. to 3:00 a.m. most days.

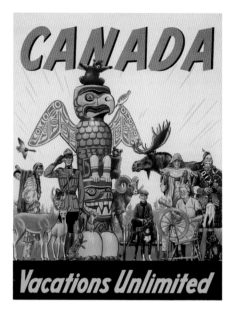

WHITE WATER RAFTING IN BANFF

The Banff region of rocky Alberta, Canada, is notorious for its world-class white water and ferocious river rapids. A wise group of travelers (we) once said that the best way to know your mountainous surroundings is to raft right through them. Grab your oars and hold on tight—we're gonna get you all Banff-ed and bothered.

Down Shit's Creek— with a Paddle

Sometimes closed off to commercial rafting companies and always gushing with dangerously extreme levels of rapids, the Kicking Horse is the only river around here really worth paddling. The river carves right through Kicking Horse Canyon in three tiers: upper, middle, and lower. Naturally, the upper canyon (and the beginning of your trip) is friendly enough to find your groove. Miles downriver, the Portage and Shotgun rapids will quickly awaken the extremist in you. From here on, the fun and games morph into panic and survival; the bottom of the middle canyon and entire lower canyon are filled with challenging rapids that often arrive unannounced. Totaling over twenty miles, with a consistent water temperature just above freezing, Kicking Horse River will quickly put some commendable rafting experience under your belt.

Keep It Classy

As you progress downriver, you'll start holding on to your oar for dear life (as you should) while smacking into Class III, IV, and even V rapids. What do these numbers mean? Quite simply, an Association of All Things Adventurous (actually called the American Whitewater organization decided to make an internationally recognized scale of how badly the water will kick your ass—aptly named the "International Scale of River Difficulty." The scale divides rapids into classes from I through VI; I being a leisurely paddle over waves that wouldn't disrupt a snorkeler's breathing; VI being a green-conscious government's alternative to the electric chair—almost certain death. Just so you know what you're diving into, the lower part of the Kicking Horse, starting with Portage and Shotgun rapids, are rated a consistent III to IV and can rush to a V during unpredictable parts of the sport's summer season. If you've got the rapids in a chokehold and your adventurous side needs more of a tickle, ask your guides to let you swim once the tour is over. Trying to backstroke down an icy-cold Class III rapid should sufficiently fire up your veins.

From mild to wild, the Kicking Horse River is easily the toughest route through the canyon. Take a one-day tour down or split the trip into a multiday excursion. However you plan to paddle, once you reach the bottom, we guarantee you'll feel like you're on top of the world.

CRACKS, CREVICES, AND CANYONING

Canyoning is one of the most extreme sports out there. The concept is simple: use all means necessary to reach the bottom of a canyon. The execution is difficult: you'll have to rappel, slide, climb, jump, and dive to make it out alive. Once you're in this bitch, there's no pulling out. You can't just roll down a canyon anywhere there's a crack. The conditions must be just right, and in Interlaken in Switzerland, you'll find the perfect balance of steep cliffs, big drops, and roaring waterfalls.

Start From the Top

Jagged rocks, unimaginable heights, freezing-cold streams, and no sign of immediate escape: This is what Interlaken has to offer. So why would anybody voluntarily do this? Because it makes you feel alive, and you can only do it (and survive) in a few places around the globe. Canyoning (known in the United States as canyoneering) has been around for thousands of years but not always as a sport. Originally, native populations found refuge, shelter, and food in the deep granite and sandstone canyons of America's west coast. It wasn't until the 1960s that death-wish adventurers started exploring the ins and outs of Mother Nature's deep, gushing crevices for sport.

What Goes Down

In Interlaken, your adventures in the canyon begin at the top of a mountain. You'll first change into protective gear and receive some brief safety guidelines (e.g., don't jump off any fifty-foot cliffs without first telling a guide), then you'll hike for a good half hour until you really feel alone in the canyon; that's when the fun begins. The first dive into the freezing mountain water effectively evaporates whatever balls you have left from the provided nut-hugging wetsuit. The next three hours consists of jumping, diving, rappelling, sliding, swimming, and shivering down the canyon with a small group of as-crazy-as-you comrades. It's an adventure of a lifetime, so you better be prepared. Tuck in your elbows as you go down nature's own paved slides; they're gonna get bumpy. Keep your knees bent on the cliff jumps; the landing pools can be shallow (remember to canyonball). Don't fuck with your carabiners; rappels are a long way down. Bring a towel; you're gonna get soaked. And definitely buy the individually edited HD video; nobody's ever gonna believe you did this.

Choose Your Canyon

Interlaken knows your time and budget are limited, so your choices are simplified thanks to three organizations—Interlaken Adventure, Outdoor Interlaken, and Alpin Center. All three offer similar rates of around $300 for the trip. Since each company specializes in one specific canyon, choosing your package depends on which canyon you decide to conquer. Some are smaller and shorter, others are terrifyingly large. If you want to go for the biggest and baddest, choose Chli Schliere. Enclosed in tight rock walls over 300 feet tall and defined by huge waterfalls, these are the tallest jumps and slides in the region. With extremely challenging 100-plus-foot rappels, this thing will quickly show you what real canyoning is all about.

FIVE WAYS TO TEAR THROUGH GLACIER COUNTRY

You won't be in Glacier Country long before you realize this place sure as shit is *not* the Shire. Fed high from the Southern Alps, the twin glaciers that define the region—Fox and Franz Josef—trade rolling hills for deep crevasses and miles of meltwater that lead into icy blue abyss. Don't go grabbing your groin for warmth just yet—we'll tell you how to keep Kiwi cool while touring New Zealand's greatest glaciers.

PADDLE ACROSS

Take to your oars and paddle a relaxing day away on New Zealand's largest unmodified wetland, Ōkārito Lagoon. The overextended toenail on the foot of the Franz Josef, Ōkārito's glass-smooth water surface will wind you through the inlets, channels, and rivers where the famously elusive white heron (properly known as kotuku) resides. If you're in the "relax when I'm dead" school of thought, kick the action into overdrive and contact Eco Rafting. These guys make blitzing your heartbeat their business. A boatload of rafting options—like heli-rafting and multi-day excursions—will put some power behind that paddle.

CLIMB THROUGH

Make the hair on your chest grow Chia Pet-fast as you rappel down glacier cracks and crevasses guided by the day's sun rays.

Ice climbing is the most popular (and most demanding) sport in the area but isn't as intimidating as it sounds. Getting a grip may feel weird at first, but rest assured that a harnessed-in team from either Franz Josef Glacier Guides or Fox Glacier Guiding will catch you if you fall. The awesome realization that you're walking on thousand-year-old water comes with the package.

HIKE BELOW

From the tip of the glaciers, down lakes, through rain forests, and toward the Tasman Sea, Glacier Country is frigidly scenic. Tons of hikes wind through the terrains and reward you with panoramic glacial views. For Franz Josef, take the Pakihi walk and listen to the haunting call of New Zealand's most endangered bird, the rowi. Mount Fox's route will get you up close and personal with Fox Glacier and simultaneously test your strength—the one mile hike up to the peak takes four hours! Do the math, and do some pull-ups in preparation.

SOAR ABOVE

Add some height to your journey by sky-diving into the damn thing. Fox Glacier's dives of 12,000 and 16,000 feet will ensure that you get your adrenaline rush and you get it good. Take in the view of the glaciers and rain forests during the flight of anticipation before you jump straight out and become part of the landscape yourself.

SINK IN

Long days of adventure can take a toll no matter how ripped and ready you think you are. Before heading back, sink into the hot pools of Franz Josef. According to local legend, the tears of Hine Hukatere, an ancient adventuress—wept for the fall of her husband during a climb—are the water source of Franz Josef Glacier. Bathe yourself gloriously in her hot misery to work out your kinks.

FIVE ALTERNATIVE USES FOR AN ICE PICK

An ice pick is a great tool to have when scaling a glacier. But what about those off days when you're just lounging around? Here are five things you can do with your extremely sharp and dangerous climbing tool:

1. Fillet a flounder.

2. Check for cavities.

3. Stab a revolutionary, especially if his last name is Trotsky or yours is Stalin.

4. Piss off a kid by popping his balloon.

5. Open letters from jail pen pals.

MUCHO MACHU PICCHU

No one knows exactly why it's there, how it was built, or what type of magic it can harness, but a trip to South America is incomplete without a climb to Machu Picchu. The world is full of overhyped tourist spots; this isn't one of them. This massive Incan complex solidly deserves its title as one of the New Seven Wonders of the World. Just sixty miles north of Cuzco, Peru, the capital city is where the mind-blowing pilgrimage begins. You can fly into Alejandro Velasco Astete International Airport, take a bus, or big pimp it and float into Peru via the Amazon.

OTP Tip: Machu Picchu sits between two mountain peaks—Huayna Picchu and Machu Picchu Montaña. Uncrust your eyes before dawn to see the clouds rising over the ancient complex from atop either peak. You can hire a guide at the park entrance should you need some early morning trekking assistance.

WHY WONDER?

American explorer Hiram Bingham found more than 100 skeletons when a local boy led him to the complex in 1911. The Incans had mysteriously constructed 140 temples, mausoleums, vaults, and houses out of giant stones with their bare hands, right into steep Andean slopes.

No one knows why the city was abandoned thousands of years ago. Some people think aliens built it to bring civilization to man; others believe its structures form a psychedelic astrological calendar.

OTP Tip: An ISIC (International Student Identity Card) will get you 50 percent off entrance admission. Tickets are only good for the day they were issued—if you oversleep, consider your cash gone.

TREK IT OUT

While Machu's downfall is shrouded in mystery, one thing is known for sure: The Incans didn't fuck around when it came to stairs. Any real trip to Machu Picchu includes 100 or so flights of uneven stone stairs to get to the complex entrance. If that doesn't set your ass on fire, you can also do a three- to five-day trek along the Urubamba River to fully earn the insane view. The Incan Trail is tried-and-true, and a spot on an organized trek with any number of agencies in Cusco will run you about $600 to $700. Prices include park entrance, a tent, food, a Peruvian guide who knows his shit, and a donkey to carry yours.

Everyone has seen the played-out pictures of Machu Picchu by now. But no picture can capture the crispness of Peruvian mountain air, the size and scale of the complex, and the deserved soreness raging through your body the next day.

OTP Tip: Ditch the crowd all together and tame those mountains with a map and sheer willpower. You don't need a permit to do the Salkanty or Choquequirao trails *sin guia* and the donkeys could use a breather.

FLOAT YOUR WAY OUT

If you've had your fill of mountains in Peru, change up the scenery by hitching a ride to Brazil via the Amazon. Much more scenic than a cloudy plane ride, the Amazon is over 4,000 miles long, can be up to twenty-five miles wide, and is filled with plants and animals even Wikipedia has a hard time describing. The major artery of South America's heart, the Amazon is sometimes the only road that connects points A and B. You can pay for a bus or a flight to get to the jungle, or milk it like a jaguar cub and get there for free. All it takes are some courage and sea legs.

The Road Less Traveled

The most-traveled route on the Amazon is from Iquitos, Peru, to Manaus, Brazil, with a connection in Leticia, Colombia. These rivers are technically tributaries of the Amazon, which begins for real in Manaus, but have plenty of piranhas, pink dolphins, tiny ports, and jungly shores to keep your senses occupied en route.

Get on a Boat!

Prep your Spanish sailor lingo and stroll on up to the port in Iquitos, flex your guns and tell them how you "worked on your uncle's sailboat that one summer." Though some boats ferry up to 600 passengers, they're primarily cargo ships that carry anything from TVs and sound systems to chickens and grains. You'll probably sacrifice your back for several days hauling cargo, but if you know your rice and beans, weaseling your way into the kitchen may be an option.

Chillin' on one of these boats is an experience that romantically sits somewhere between a no-holds-barred jungle safari and an eighteenth-century prison ship. Catch some gnarly bugs, learn a couple samba moves, and drink your way into a Peruvian sunset. You will sleep in a hammock on the deck and love every moment of your successful labor-for-travel trade.

HIKE UP YOUR KILT FOR AN EXTREME STROLL

A nation that normally lets it all hang out, Scotland has many best-kept secrets, one of which is the ninety-six-mile hike through Rob Roy country along the West Highland Way (WHW). The "Way" begins in Milngavie (pronounced Mul Guy) just north of Glasgow and ends in downtown Fort William at a statue of a man rubbing his tired Scottish feet. The trek will take you through Grimm's fairy tale–like forests, around the banks of bonnie Loch Lomond, up steep and rocky hillsides, across farms with curious sheep, and deep into the eerie and isolated Rannoch Moor.

THE WAY

Most trekkers head out in May when the weather is best, the baby lambs are rambunctious, and the midges (small mosquito-y bugs that swarm and bite the bloody hell out of you) aren't prevalent. For a more extreme trek, schedule your hike in the winter with gale-force winds and snowdrifts that obscure the path. An ice pick, instead of a hippie walking stick, is recommended during this time.

If hiking ninety-six miles isn't enough, you can tack on another crazy seventy-nine miles along the Great Glen Way and cuddle with the Loch Ness Monster, who presumably hangs out in Inverness, the hike's endpoint. There are also plenty of day trips along the way, such as climbing Ben Nevis and Ben Lomond, as well as several other Munros (a Scottish mountain with a height over 3,000 feet).

The Way of the Way

An unspoken mandate of the West Highland Way is to stuff yourself stupid on hearty Scottish food while covering those daily half- (and sometimes full-) marathon distances. One of the iconic landmarks near Loch Lomond is the 300-year-old pub, the Drovers Inn.

This haunted, tumble-down establishment is where cattle drovers stopped for a pint and some haggis as they moved their cattle down from the Highlands for sale and export. Vegetarians wanting to try the local fare can order the neeps and tatties vegetarian haggis, or Scotch broth soup.

The Rowardennan Hotel, another stop along the Way, offers up a meal with a view overlooking the eastern shores of Loch Lomond. The food tastes like manna, and the beer is perfect for washing down your blister-numbing ibuprofen. If your feet call it quits, the hotel offers cheap bunk beds to hold you over until you feel Braveheart-good again.

SLEEP FOR FREE

While staying at bed-and-breakfasts is an option, it's cheaper (and more fun) to pitch a tent and camp your way through the hike. Per Scottish law, wild camping is allowed except in places where it is posted otherwise—specifically Rannoch Moor—as long as you pick up after your grizzly self and use a civilized camp stove. If indoor plumbing sounds attractive every once in a while, there are designated campsites (with food options nearby) and hostels scattered along the trail, as well.

If you're partial to pristine streams, mossy pine forests, views of Scottish lochs, and glimpses of feral goats and shaggy cows, coupled with giant blisters, missing toenails, and burning muscles, pull up your man-skirt and get trekking.

WHAT THE F*CK iS HAGGIS?

People consume some pretty nasty shit on planet Earth. From black pudding in the UK (not chocolaty in the least) to baby mice wine in Korea, the gag factor is sky-high. Always up for competition, the Scots throw their hat into the ring with haggis, a national treasure you'll soon learn to puke up with Scottish pride.

What the "Pluck"?

Haggis is made up of sheep's "pluck," or the heart, liver, and lungs of Mary's little lamb. Chefs mash them up with onions, oatmeal, suet, and spices, and moisten the mash with stock before shoving it into the animal's emptied stomach, at which point, it's simmered in stock for about three hours before being dumped onto the plates of hungry, red-faced Scots. Haggis is a lot like sausage, and people love its reputed nutty texture and savory flavor.

Hag-Story

The first written haggis recipe is from 1430 Lancashire in Northwest England, so the nasty train to Haggisville has been pulling in and out of the station for a long-ass time. Haggis got so popular that in 1787, Robert Burns wrote a poem about it. His "Address to Haggis" points out that true connoisseurs will eat it with "neeps and tatties," yellow turnips or rutabagas and boiled and mashed potatoes. Today, people eat it with whatever they want and wash it down with Scotch, a pint of beer, or whatever alcohol is around to effectively neutralize the taste of sheep insides.

Hag on This

Scottish restaurants have interpreted haggis in all sorts of ways. In snooty restaurants, try the "Flying Scotsman," a chicken breast hugging a lump of haggis. And since everything is better with bacon, when the "Flying Scotsman" puts on a bacon kilt, you have the dish known as "Chicken Balmoral." Just when you vegetarians thought you were off the hook, since the '60s, vegetarian haggis has been produced with vegetables and various other fillings. Step into a supermarket in Scotland, and you'll have your pick of the haggis litter. You can also get your intestinal fix in a can (like Scottish Spam).

At the Scottish dinner table, the "when in Rome" school of thinking absolutely applies. Haggis is as popular as *Braveheart*, and filling your stomach with other stomachs is almost mandatory. Talk to the big white telephone should the innards want out.

GET HIGH, GET LOW, GET SCARED

Most thrill-seeking backpackers first experience Africa by way of South Africa, a country that mashes together some of the best extreme adventures available worldwide. Sure you can Jeep around on a safari, but here are three equally amazing ways to work at least one near-death experience into your trip.

GET HIGH: TABLE MOUNTAIN

Have yourself an adrenaline picnic atop Cape Town's Table Mountain, a landmark you can either admire from the beach, take a cable car to ascend, or climb like a rabid beast. Tackle the tougher (adorably named) routes such as Double Jeopardy or Mary Poppins and Her Great Umbrella to prove your prowess. Once your feet are on the mountain's defining plateau (the "table"), peek through the tablecloth of clouds to get tasty views of the Indian and Atlantic oceans, Robben Island (where Mandela was imprisoned), and all of Cape Town. If your inner junkie hungers for more, have yourself an abseiling adventure and rappel off the side of the mountain. Ropes chaffing your baby-bottom? Diving into Kamikaze Canyon's natural pools should fix you right up.

To nail down unique sleeping arrangements, rev your flaccid calves and take on the Hoerikwaggo Trail from Table Mountain to Cape Point, which includes a stop in the Orange Kloof Forest. While wild camping is forbidden on Table Mountain, you can

spend the night in one of the designated camp areas at Orange Kloof Tented Camps on a trail starting from the Silvermine Dam. These camps hook you up with everything you need so you can pass out under the Table, safari-style.

GET LOW: SURFING SOUTH AFRICA

In South Africa, people don't just catch waves, they hunt down massive, rolling aqua giants and shred them apart, savoring every bubbling bit. Show off your mad surfing skills by tearing through some of the best waves in the world. For surfing near Cape Town, grab the commuter rail out to Muizenberg, where you can rent wetsuits and boards (and instruction if you need it). Keep your head above water and your ears open for shark sirens.

To get deep into the local surf culture, head to Jeffreys Bay (JBay to the natives), near Port Elizabeth. You won't find too many tourists (unless you go during the Billabong surf festival in July), but you will find enough waves to slap you silly until the sun goes down.

To tackle the biggest breed of wave around, head to Dungeons in Hout Bay. Thirty-foot swells are on the menu at Cape Hout, which is best reached by boat from nearby Cape Town. Successfully tackling these demons will put you up there with the pros who've competed here for Red Bull's Big Wave Africa events.

GET SCARED: SHARK DIVING TILL YOU CRAP YOURSELF

If the shark tunnel at the local aquarium is the closest you've been to a Great White, get ready to loosen your bowels with the terrifying fun of shark cage diving in the waters of South Africa, where the finned fishies swim. Most expeditions leave from Gansbaai, a fishing village near "Shark Alley." The Alley is a narrow channel between two small islands where sharks love to chomp on the Cape fur seals that congregate in the area. No need to be dive-certified—just make sure you have an intense desire to piss in a wetsuit when a Great White slams up against the cage.

THE WORLD'S FIVE MOST CHALLENGING MOUNTAINS TO CLIMB

These peaks don't care if you have the agility of a rhesus monkey, the sticky toes of a tree frog, or arms like Arnold; they will gloriously ravage you to the core regardless. Checking any one of these mountains off your climbing list will instantly elevate you to the status of climbing royalty.

Mount Everest–Nepal
(8,850 meters)

Nickname: Listen, it's like the Chuck Norris of mountains, so a nickname would be beneath it.
Famous for: highest mountain peak in the world

Baintha Brakk–Pakistan
(7,285 meters)

Nickname: "The Ogre"
Famous for: almost vertical ascent (its South Face rises 3,000 meters across only 2000 meters); craggy as can be; most bear-infested camp areas

Kilimanjaro–Tanzania
(5,895 meters)

Nickname: "The Roof of Africa"
Famous for: highest in Africa; comprised of three volcanoes; not that hard to climb, but a legendary trek

Fitzroy–Border of Chile and Argentina,
Andes (3,375 meters)

Nickname: "Frigid Fitzgerald"
Famous for: not a grower or a shower, just icy as fuck, avalanche-prone, and jagged; averages only one ascent per year

K2–border of China and Pakistan
(8,612 meters)

Nickname: "The Savage"
Famous for: second-highest peak in the world; second-highest fatality rate (one out of every four people die trying to reach the summit); has never been climbed in the winter

CAMPING IN THE JUNGLE

Right on Colombia's Caribbean coast is the tropical jungle reserve of Tayrona National Park. Colorful flowers, trees with surfboard-size leaves, monkeys, lizards, hundreds of bird species (we caught Toucan Sam red-nosedly snooping through our pack), and even jaguars live up the mountains and down by the beaches of this Colombian paradise. With cheap hammocks, huts, and tents up for rent, you can take up residence, too.

CHOOSE YOUR CAMPGROUNDS

Tayrona is a wildly popular destination for backpackers looking to explore, party, and relax just like you. Being a natural reserve, you can't just plop your ass wherever. Thankfully, three sections for camping keep your options simple.

Cañaveral is the closest campsite near the entrance of the park—it can actually be reached by car. Known for its $275/night beachfront Eco-Habs, Cañaveral rents $20 nightly tents near the beach with surprisingly clean showers and shitters to boot.

Arrecifes is a one-hour hike through the jungle from the tip of Cañaveral. Once you make it, Bukaru is your best bet for camping with hammocks, tents, and cabanas available from $12 a night. As beautiful as Arrecifes' beaches are, they're deemed unswimmable by the park due to the ocean's rapidly changing strong currents.

Cabo San Juan is the place to be, and it's another hour deeper than Arrecifes. If you're lugging loads of stuff, rent a horse and have it do your hauling for $18. Sleep in a sheltered hammock by the beach for $12, try a tent for a few more, or bring your own and sleep for $9 a night. Whichever way you sleep, your days will be spent like they should be: eating good food at the campground's restaurant, living among awesome wildlife, and relaxing on the sandy beach.

PREPARE FOR PARADISE

Santa Marta's a half hour drive away from Tayrona National Park and it's $20 to enter. Here are a few tips to make sure you're geared up and ready to stay before setting up camp.

- Water: You need it. Tayrona's got it, but it's damn expensive ($5 for 1.5 liters). Stock up on bottles before entering and guzzle away.

- Unlike America, park cops are no laughing matter here. Plastic bags are not permitted and will be taken. Drugs will also be confiscated. You can buy alcohol in the park, and as for the rest–conceal at your own caution.

- Food is available but canned and bagged goods are a great way to save money.

- Flashlights are a must so you don't end up in the wrong tent at night. Sneaky tricksters.

- Toiletries will keep you from looking like a castaway, burning in the sun, or getting turned into bug breakfast.

- Snorkeling gear will save you from haggling with local beach vendors.

- A sleeping bag or a mosquito net will give you the upper hand during your nightly battles for sleep.

- If you want to try your hand at being sneaky to avoid the entrance fee, there are three side entry spots–namely, Mexico (a village, not the country), Calabazo, and Los Naranjos–that have proven successful for other travelers.

FILL YOUR DAYS

With seventy square miles spanning over two completely different ecosystems—mountain and sea—Parque Tayrona won't short you on stuff to see and do.

One with the Sea

You can swim everywhere along the Park's coast *except* Arrecifes. All the beaches are insanely beautiful, and protected Caribbean coral with colorful fish also make for great snorkeling. Bonus: there's a nudist beach.

OTP Tip: While a few camp "restaurants" may have you thinking otherwise, the dining at Cabo San Juan is better than decent. Go for a $5 spaghetti plate or try a local ceviche-fish soup, always caught fresh from the ocean you've been swimming in.

Mountain Magic

Hiking is a good way to dig deep into the inner beauty of this preserved park. Venture a few hours beyond Cabo San Juan until you reach the ancient town of Pueblito. If the archaeological ruins of a small, ancient civilization don't interest you, maybe the surrounding beaches and sounds of the Colombian jungle will.

Rumble in the Jungle

Parties are more eventful in the dark. The most nightlife you'll find in Tayrona is around a campfire where local musicians rock out to traditional tunes. Serious amounts of alcohol are consumed and the rest of the night is up to you—just know that those beachside hammocks can support two.

THE SOUTHERN EXTREMITY

If vigorous tango dancing isn't enough to shed the meat-feasting pounds you put on in Buenos Aires, it's time to head south—all the way south—to the southernmost city in the world. Ushuaia, the ice-cold heart of Tierra del Fuego, is your adrenaline nerve center in this rugged remote tip of Patagonia. Light a match under your *parilla*-enlarged ass and burn through the "Land of Fire."

TIERRA DEL FUEGO NATIONAL PARK

Tackle the Americas' southern tip in Tierra del Fuego National Park, where remembering you're at the Earth's end is easy. You rarely see another soul deep in the 240-square-mile *Into the Wild*-esque terrain. The park replaces human contact with mountains, glaciers, forests, waterfalls, and lakes all perfect for hiking, climbing, fishing, and good old-fashioned, nonmasturbatory alone time.

KAYAK THE BEAGLE CHANNEL

The rough, frigid waters of the Beagle Channel are often sailed, but jump in a lesser boat (like a kayak) to get closer to the wildlife here. Sea lions swim alongside your kayak, the albatross circle appears overhead, and penguins stand at attention on shore. You can navigate your seacraft through icebergs and watch giant ice chunks calve off glaciers into the channel. Charles Darwin cruised this waterway on the trip where he started asking questions that, still to this day, piss off school boards across the Bible Belt.

CLIMB THE MARTIAL GLACIER

Back in the day, this entire island was one monster glacier. Nowadays, only a few chunks remain. The Martial Glacier is just outside of Ushuaia and can be climbed in one good day's hike. Bypass the ski lift that shuttles old people to the glacier's base and attack the steep hour-and-a-half trail on foot. From here, you can climb up and around the glacier to get postcard views of Ushuaia and the Beagle Channel. There are signs warning you not to do this without a guide, but let's just say you can't read Spanish, gringo. Best of all, the entire day is completely free.

GO EVEN SOUTH-ER

You've come this far—why stop now? Ushuaia is the main launching point for cruises to Antarctica and if you need this one last pin to stick in your world map, this is where you start. It may be hard fitting this trip under your credit card limit, but if you can scrounge up the change somehow (bake sale?) you'll be able to cruise among whales, cut through massive icebergs, get pummeled by unforgiving waves on Zodiacs rafts, hike across jagged glaciers, march with penguin colonies, and get chased by sea lions on this land that man has yet to fuck up. Seven countries claim territory on the uninhabited continent. Stick your own flag into the southern final frontier.

WHY IT'S
ASS-COLD IN THE
LAND OF FIRE

In 1520, Ferdinand Magellan passed through a strait in the southern tip of South America. En route, he spotted many fires on the land near the huts of the indigenous people. With his creative juices flowing, Magellan named the island group the "Land of Fire," or "Tierra del Fuego" in Spanish. Despite the ass-crippling cold and without any input from the island's 10,000 year-long residents, Magellan's misnomer stuck.

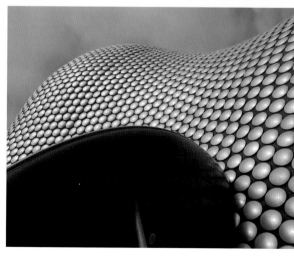

ART AND DESIGN

Explore art outside of the museum box. Graffiti, large-scale murals, sculpture, and creative multimedia integration is what our generation calls art, and the world is bursting with visual stimulation. Hit New York for a face full of graffiti, Tokyo for head-to-toe tat culture, and Amsterdam to pay a visit to the slithery snake wrapped around town. From the traditional museums of Paris to the makeshift studios of gritty Berlin, the street art culture of New York City to Gaudí's twisted Sagrada Família, the multitude of ways people express themselves around the world will stir you with inspiration—and maybe expand your definition of art.

COLOR THROUGH THE HAZE

Amsterdam's street art is funky, trippy, and guaranteed to tickle your creativity. Sure you could spend your time trapped in musty museums, but why not breathe in some of that bracing North Sea air and check out the graffiti bombings around town instead? In a city of greats like Van Gogh and Rembrandt, street art is embraced as another form of fine art, just with a different medium and a more solid canvas. Leave the tourists to the Museumplein and find yourself among the avant garde of today's times under Amsterdam's bridges.

ROOTED IN PUNK

While painting on walls is caveman-years old, Amsterdam's street art materialized in the early 1970s. Graffiti artists, also known as writers or bombers, emerged from the European punk movement, using graffiti as a way to express discontent with the troubling political and economic climate during that time. Earlier artworks focused more on political activism and rebellious poetry, while modern Amsterdam writers explore typography as a medium of expression. When you're prepping for your trip, you can write your entire itinerary in the download-able font appropriately named "Amsterdam Graffiti."

The Amsterdam municipal government has recently attempted to decriminalize graffiti by creating legal opportunities to paint in specially designated areas. The government is also working to legitimize some of the better-known artists by sponsoring or commissioning them, promoting their exhibitions, and even purchasing some of their works for museums.

THE HANDS THAT ROCK THE SPRAY CAN

Niels "Shoe" Meulman

The Bill Shakespeare of graffiti, Niels began tagging as "Shoe" in 1979 and achieved legendary status by the time he was eighteen. In the '80s, he formed an international graffiti crew—"Crime Time Kings"—with Bando from Paris and Mode2 from London. He transitioned to legit graphic design in the '90s, running his own firm, but remained rooted in the street art scene and is dropping shit to this day. Shoe's distinctive style is known as Calligraffiti—a mash-up of calligraphy and graffiti—and he has recently released an eponymous book of his work.

Ottograph

If you have a velvet Andy Warhol print and an ironic lava lamp, you'll love Ottograph, whose pop art influences can be seen all over Amsterdam. Ottograph began tagging at the age of ten and his vibrant graffiti is rich in social commentary, but not so cerebral you need to smoke a joint to understand it . . . although, it could enhance the experience.

Mickey

Mickey developed as a writer by scribbling names on any available surface. Her current street art has characteristic eyeballs and aliens embedded around the paintings, which, as she puts it, "watch the world." Her day job is teaching second-grade future taggers.

DHM

Hugo Mulder, a.k.a. DHM, is like Spider-Man —graphic designer by day, bomb-dropper by night. You'll soon begin to recognize the black-and-white tattoo style he's been crafting since the mid-'80s, which covers stretches of the city.

X Streets Collective

A crew of talented artists with diverse styles, the collective includes notables such as Ives. The creative director of Project Amsterdam Street Art, Ives is an artist that emerged into the street art scene in the mid-'90s to beautifully combine stencil and freehand. Like the Justice League of street art, other members of X Streets—namely BUSTart, Zaira, Skatin Chinchilla, MLSS, Karma83, and Seifrei—merge their talents to create complex and diverse murals.

TOP ART SPOTS

Henxs

To mingle with the local artists and get a tag-a-long, head over to Henxs, a small shop near the Waterlooplein, whose clientele wear masks to avoid fume inhalation and balaclavas to hide their faces from the police. You can ask them how to contact bombers and where to find some of the hidden gems of Amsterdam.

Flevopark

Head east of the city to Flevopark where you can soak up the sun and visit some of the city's vibrant bombs. If you fancy trying your hand at writing your name, the walls under the freeway in the skate park near Flevopark are all legal.

Red Light District

If you want art with a side of nudity, you can find graffiti in the Red Light District. One noteworthy mural of the ladies is on Dollebegijnensteeg near the canal. Make sure you venture over to Spuistraat where you can see a giant Technicolor serpent coiled around an entire Dutch row house. Your trouser snake is no match for this thirty-footer.

TOO MUCH ART, NEED MORE SEX?

You can only gaze at so many *Starry Nights* before your thoughts circle back to sex. In addition to all the other sexiness characteristic to Amsterdam, it's also home to Muse du Sexe–the oldest sex museum in the world. The display cases in the *Venustempel* (Venus Temple) are full of ancient toys and wax figures of Mata Hari and her partners. When the seventeenth-century building was reclaimed in 1985, an antique, erect Hermes figurine was found in the rubble and you can have a look-see while resting comfortably on the museum's cushioned benches. It's a full-sensory experience, with muffled naughty noises pumped in through the walls. Don't miss the photo op between two massive boners. Displays of sex through the ages have cultural value–and where else could you see a medieval statue of Satan with a hard-on? This hornifying activity only costs 4 euros, which would only buy you a set of blue balls in the Red Light District.

GAUDÍ-LAND

Catalan traditionalists love their fine art museums, and the street kids deck out the cityscape with incredible murals. Local artists are constantly at work, creating mind-bending pieces that build on their artistic history and move it forward. But while many styles and expressions exist in this undoubtedly artsy city, nothing sets Barcelona visually apart from the world more than the architectural contributions of Antoni Gaudí, Barcelona's deranged master of plaster. His drippy, twisted buildings puncture the otherwise classic Spanish city blocks and turn them into stare-worthy attractions.

SOLITUDE BUILDS CHARACTER

All of that quirk definitely came from somewhere. Antoni Gaudí was born in 1852 in Reus and was a sickly kid with rheumatism (creaky joints), which forced him to sit around and look at shit by himself instead of interacting with other kids. Since walking was difficult, Tony rode a donkey and spent his early days observing animals and nature. A vegetarian for most of his life, his respect for nature shone through everything he did. Not surprisingly, he was never much of a people-person and is rumored to have died a seventy-three-year-old virgin.

LEARNING THE RULES TO BEND

Gaudí first came to Barcelona in 1868 to study architecture and, even though he was a pretty shitty student, managed to graduate and leave a lasting impression. As is often the case with weirdos, Gaudí's professors thought he was either a complete moron or a total genius. The city of Barcelona took a chance on Gaudí and commissioned him to design lampposts for the Plaça Reial. Although you could blink and miss them, the art nouveau lamps are still lighting the way today. We're betting on genius.

CASA VICENS

With the lampposts, Gaudí gained some serious street cred and was commissioned to build a house for a rich family that owned a ceramic tile factory. From 1883 to 1888, Gaudí worked on Casa Vicens, drawing from his fascination with Oriental details and Moorish architecture to create the ridiculous McMansion. As a tribute to the man who paid him, Gaudí detailed the casa

with the owner's multicolor tiles, which made the whole thing look like a shimmering fish at sunrise. His next projects continued to decorate the city with architectural weirdness. In 1910, he completed Casa Milà, which resembles stone waves; it was almost too damn weird for the government's approval. Inspired by nature, Gaudí's geometrically defying designs can be seen in many other buildings around town, like the Casa Calvet and Casa Batlló. Park Güell is an entire park of surrealist sculptures and structures, perching high above the city like a tripped-out thought bubble.

SAGRADA FAMÍLIA

A Catholic bordering on fanatic, Gaudí dedicated most of his adult life to designing a church that would scare the bejesus out of Jesus. Gaudí began working on Sagrada Família—the most famous site in Barcelona—in 1882, and it's *still* not finished. The dripping, curling towers hit you in the face as you walk out of the train station, and your eyes take a few minutes to adjust to its insanely unique design. Part Gothic, part

Naturalistic, and all Gaudí, Sagrada Família is so intricate and complex that dozens of architects and builders are still working to realize Gaudí's vision, over 130 years after construction began.

DEATH BY TROLLEY

An artist through and through, old man Gaudí was one of those famous guys who dressed like a bum to prove a point. Gaudí was struck by a tram in Barcelona in 1926 and, since he looked less than decent, was given the kind of medical attention homeless people get (i.e., sideways looks and a Band-Aid). When it was discovered that he wasn't a mere (human!) hobo, Gaudí was asked if he wished to be transferred to a better facility, but he declined. After several days in a crappy hospital, Gaudí succumbed to his injuries and died. Point proven. Lesson learned? Listen to your mom and always wear clean underwear because you never know when you'll get hit by a trolley and be mistaken for a homeless person.

DALÍ MUSEUM: FIGUERES

Just north of Barcelona, in Figueres, lies the surrealistic tribute to Salvador Dalí, another wacky original. This theater-turned-museum was curated by the talented media whore himself and contains important pieces from every stage of his twisted artistic life.

Here, you will find the long-legged elephants, dripping doodles, and funky jewelry that best characterize Dalí's style. The Mae West Room, in which art and interior design meld together like the colors in a lava lamp, will bend your mind into submission. Born in Figueres, Dalí made damn sure this museum gave his hometown something to be proud of. The city itself is tiny and has a half-block stretch that resembles La Rambla for ants. Great for day-trip tripping—give Sal a holla when you roll through; his crypt has been chillin' in the center of the museum since 1989.

5 BEST
PLACES TO LEARN
SPANiSH

Four hundred twenty-three million people speak Spanish around the world, and once you leave the comfort of the classroom, you'll realize that everyone has their own version and learning just the basics will never suffice. Get elbow-deep in conjugations, absorb ridiculous local slang, and relish in the kind of knowledge only travelingcan buy. Put away the textbooks and immerse yourself in a Spanish-speaking destination to really figure out the inner-workings of the language. Each of these unique destinations has its own Spanish flare and plenty of perks to keep you chatting till your mouth goes dry.

Andalucia, Spain
Fastest

Any of the regions down in the south of Spain are fast-talking slur fests. It will sound like total gibberish at first but their turbo tongues will force you into learning overdrive if you want to survive socially. The study abroad programs in Cordoba and Seville are well established and great for getting a wrangle on the basics (just note, most classes are taught completely in Spanish). Swallow your syllables, familiarize yourself with tapas and day-drinking, and acquire that (debatably) sexy lisp at lightening speed.

Buenos Aires, Argentina
Poshiest

Often referred to as the "Paris of the South," Buenos Aires might be a little fancy, but luckily, there's really nothing French about them, including their native language. Since BsAs is the most popular gateway for backpackers to the rest of South America, there are many established programs around that'll help you learn Spanish (sometimes in exchange for teaching English). If starting up a convo in Spanish gives you anxiety, this city has all kinds of lubricants—wine, tango, and *fútbol*, to name a few—to get the words flowing. And after all is said and done, you can always partake in a little *siesta* to clear your mind.

Havana, Cuba
Danciest

If you have a hard time communicating with your lips, get the point across with your hips. Music is a universal language and Cubans hold the highest level of proficiency. Cuba is an excellent place to learn Spanish because they live their lives on the streets, and constant mingling creates a strong sense of community. Cubans are a loud bunch and you'll never endure awkward silences no matter how thick the language barrier may be. When you're done wrapping your mouth around the language, stick a cigar in it and suck down the smoke of success.

Puebla, Mexico
Best Slang

The fourth-largest city in Mexico, Puebla pumps out all kinds of textiles and attracts many students to the Spanish Institute of Puebla due to its rich history and thriving economy. It's filled with incredible architecture that spans eras and styles, has some of the most beautiful churches and cathedrals, and is the origin of the stick-to-your-face mole poblano. Studying Spanish here will help you acquire all the necessary Mexican slang that'll make sense when you get back home. In your downtime, go see the ruins of nearby Cholula; there are some great pre-Columbian pyramids and thoughts of hot sauce will run through your mind all day.

Granada, Nicaragua
Most Options

Well-established language programs are available at local universities in both Granada and the less-touristy Leon. You don't need to know your past participles from your progressives to enroll and the locals are eager to talk you in their native tongue. Want some surfing with your Spanish? Nica's surfing culture is incredible and we can't think of a better way to break through the language barrier than bonding over a few ripping waves.

OTP Tip: To rest your ears from all the chatter, hop to Ometepe, a little piece of secluded paradise that's quickly disappearing on Lake Nicaragua.

GRITTY ART, WAREHOUSE SPACES, AND STREET STYLES

Breaking free from its Wall-divided days, Berlin is united through its artistic expression. Like the city itself, art in Berlin is innovative, unconventional, and constantly changing with the creative, free spirits of its people who fight control by coloring the machine's monotony. One part raw, one part refined, and all parts real, Berlin's explosive art scene will inspire you to get your hands dirty.

GRITTY ART

After a lengthy period of historic oppression, the progressively liberal trend that plows forward today is voiced and displayed through the creative artists who live, breathe, and decorate Berlin. Their art tells the tale of a city transcending its past and flourishing in its freedom. As such, themes can cover everything from societal chaos to peace, prosperity, and community. This means that you're as likely to find a portrayal of a decapitated cat's head cooking in an oven as you are a building-size depiction of East and West Berliners uniting. Most will be raunchy; all will be nice.

WAREHOUSE SPACES

The beauty of Berlin is that it's still coming up. A new player in a long-established game, Berlin isn't yet influenced by the poshness and snobbery sometimes associated with art. Exhibits and venues are as down-to-earth as the artists. You'll find dozens of dilapidated buildings inhabited

by starving artists showcasing their work all throughout the city, especially in the district of Mitte. Walk right in and look around; each room has a different flavor, and most of the works are for sale. In SOX, you'll find an all-outdoors gallery on Oranien Street in Kreuzberg. Window-shopping at its finest, the tiny window space (only a few yards wide) switches up its showcase every few weeks.

STREET STYLES

Berlin is hailed as the mecca of urban art. First thrown up in the '60s in response to the creation of the Berlin Wall, street art has shifted from cries for equality to mind-fucking murals that turn the city's streets into colorful canvases portraying the political progression. The biggest in the international game—Banksy, Invader, and Blu, to name just a few—have sprayed their marks on Berlin, alongside the works of local guys like El Bocho, Alias, and XOOOOX. Lucky for you, finding street art in Berlin is as easy as finding decent schnitzel around town. For a sure thing, walk along the East Side Gallery, the largest (just under a mile long), still-standing segment of the Wall painted by dozens of artists as a freedom memorial.

Currently controlled, inhabited, and decorated by the people, Berlin is like that first college apartment where all your artsy friends got drunk and drew in your hallway, except there's no deposit to worry about.

CHEFCHAOUEN

MOROCCO'S BLUE CITY

Like a Smurf village nestled into the Rif mountains, Chefchaouen looks like the sky dipped down for a minute and stained the buildings blue. Close to Tangier, this city has been in a tug-of-war with Spain for centuries, and hints of Spanish architecture and art mix into the Moroccan motif here. Nothing in Morocco's blue city will ever leave you feeling gray.

BEHIND THE BLUE

The Spanish Inquisition force-fed Christianity to anyone and everyone in its path and left many Muslims and Jews scrambling for a place to call home. Moriscos and Marranos—or Christian-converted Muslims and Jews, respectively—settled here alongside Berber tribespeople to duck out from the Spanish. In existence since 1471, Chefchaouen has always been a hideout where beliefs all blend to blue.

While pretty to look at, the town's distinct hue isn't aesthetically motivated. The blue comes from Jewish teachings, which say that this magical hue, when interwoven in prayer shawls, keeps you connected to God. From the looks of it, the good people of Chefchaouen have a 5G connection.

TO DO IN BLUE

As is true for many parts of Morocco, this city is split in two. The old *medina* with its punch of red terra-cotta tiles, contains the kasbah—a fortress that houses a garden, museum and art gallery—and the Grand Mosque, an octagonal mosque closed to non-Muslims but nonetheless, a wonder to peep from outside. The new city, the center of which is Plaza Mohammed V, which was designed by Spanish artist Joan Miró.

Tagines made with those punch-you-in-the-buds spices are the specialty here and their goat cheese—a boldly flavored creamy curd—is a tourist attraction in and of itself. The blue city walls provide an enticing

> *Fun Fact*
>
> Aside from religious reasons, as a bonus, painting the walls blue seems to repel mosquitos. Win-win.

background to the colorful goods on sale, like one-of-a-kind wool garments, carpets, and intricate ceramics.

All hikes through the hills, where you'll experience sweeping views of the all blue surroundings cradled by the Mediterranean ocean, start at Chefchaouen. These strolls take you through little villages, thick greenery, and around mountain streams. At night, constellations come alive in the clear sky to remind you that we all see the same stars . . . except the people of Chefchaouen get to see the unobstructed-by-smog version.

GREENS IN THE BLUE

Let's not forget that the blue city sits inside the green Rif mountains; as in the kind of green you smoke. "Chefchaouen" means "watch the horns," which speaks to the goat-horned mountain peaks behind the city. And when you're high on their supply, those goats really come to life. For more on taking a good Moroccan toke, check out page 134.

FIVE COOLEST UNESCO WORLD HERITAGE SITES

Ever wondered how you get your impressive lawn sculpture to be a protected world heritage site? For starters, you'll have to compete with places like the Taj Mahal, Ankgor Wat, and the following five incredible UNESCO sites.

Longmen Grottoes, China

The grottiest grottoes in the world, this site contains a huge collection of Chinese stone carvings of Buddhist art set into rocky holes along the banks of the Yihe River. Hef doesn't stand a chance.

Lord Howe Island Group, Australia

A group of volcanic islands, the land here is filled with the kinds of animals and plants Americans fear. Plus, if you're flying over them and look closely, the islands resemble shark teeth.

The Rideau Canal, Canada

Bike lanes are cool, but picture a frozen skateway that you can ice-skate for five continuous miles. This is just that, with hot chocolate stands on the side as a bonus.

Royal Palaces of Abomey, Benin

Talk of vanished kingdoms really gets our juices flowing, and this shell of a kingdom that once was is complete with curvy animal sculptures and eerily empty palace rooms.

Himeji-jo, Japan

A grouping of white castles dating back to 1333 that look like they're floating in the clouds, not only do they contain Japan's largest castle live but–according to a handful of legends–also many a ghost.

MAGNIFICENT STRUCTURES

Mother Russia has been busy building incredible structures for centuries. Moscow's architecture is a mix of old and new, with a majestic collection of clustered domes, skyscrapers, fortresses, and creative homes that'll take your breath away (if the cold doesn't snatch it first). These are a few of Moscow's most magnificent structures to get you started on your exploration of Russia's eclectic take on architecture.

ST. BASIL'S CATHEDRAL

Sittin' pretty in the Red Square with its iconic bulbous spires, St. Basil's looks like it was built by a master sand castle crafter using many buckets and shaping tools. Ivan the Terrible had the structure built in 1561 and architect Postnik Yakovlev was chosen for the job, but little else is known—except that Ivan may have had Postnik's eyes removed postconstruction so that he would never again make anything as beautiful. So it goes. When first erected, St. Basil's was a solid white with gold domes and flare in the form of helmeted, multicolored, and patterned onion domes. A new bell tower and various structures were added throughout the centuries. St. Basil's—a nickname taken after the "holy fool" Basil that's buried under it—was almost destroyed by Stalin because it got in the way of his massive parades on the Red Square.

Fun Fact

If you were to check its ID, you'd find that the cathedral's real name is "The Cathedral of the Intercession of the Virgin by the Moat."

BOLSHOI THEATRE

With its towering Pantheon aesthetic, the Bolshoi Theatre is as statuesque as the Russian ballerinas that have been twirling inside it since 1780. The theater—then called the Petrovsky Theatre—was first erected by Prince Pyotr Urusov and his business bro Englishman Michael Maddox, but when the duo fell into debt, it was transferred to the government. The theatre went up in flames in 1805, was rebuilt, and then again burned to shit in 1812 during Russia's battle with Napoleon. In 1825, the theater's architects decided to go big (i.e., "Bolshoi") rather than go home. The Bolshoi Theatre was rebuilt as a massive venue for Russia's most talented troupes, with sweeping staircases and a lavish auditorium that could accommodate 2,000 ballet-goers. But the Bolshoi wasn't in the clear just yet: it burned down again in 1853, was rebuilt, succumbed to decay, was used as a gathering place for the propaganda-spewing Bolsheviks during the Soviet Union, was hit by a bomb in 1941, and underwent major reconstruction throughout the early 2000s to achieve its current immaculate glow. If that's not some resilient shit, we don't know what is!

=== *Fun Fact* ===

For fifty years, a golden curtain with the USSR symbol served as Bolshoi Theatre's main stage curtain.

MELNIKOV HOUSE

Lesser known but nonetheless magnificent, this one-of-a-kind house was built by 1920's avant-garde architect Konstantin Melnikov. It looks like a fallen water tower with punched-out hexagonal window holes, but there's so much more than meets the eye. The interior is a completely transformative experience, with light entering in patterns like a kaleidoscope and bouncing off the curved walls, wooden floors, and sculpted staircases. The house represents a unique form of architecture unseen in the rest of Russia. Sadly, while plans to turn the house into a museum are being considered, it is quickly crumbling.

THE KREMLIN

This "fortress inside a city" is how Russia does the White House. It's comprised of immaculate structures including four cathedrals, five palaces, and a massive

enclosing wall that contains the Kremlin Towers. The Kremlin's famous residents have included dukes, tsars, Catherine the Great, Stalin, and Lenin. The Kremlin was a comfortable place from which to run the Soviet Union. The Grand Kremlin Palace alone has over 700 rooms and currently houses the country's president—who, if it were up to us, would be riding around that thing in a hovercraft all day long.

Fun Fact

Inside the Kremlin, the Ivan the Great Bell Tower—with its all-white, gold-dome-topped facade—is said to be the exact center of Moscow.

GUM DEPARTMENT STORE

The GUM looks more like a place where you get your wrists whacked with a ruler for disobeying the headmaster than a store. GUM is an abbreviation derived from Russian which stands for "state universal market" and is the name given to many of the Soviet era stores where people cashed in their government-issued coupons for goods (i.e., stood in endless bread lines). Moscow's GUM, which is now ironically a department store, faces the Red Square and is the largest in the country. The ceiling is all glass, and the breathtaking interior is made from various materials like granite, marble, and limestone. The body of Stalin's wife—who committed suicide in 1932—was displayed here when Stalin used the space as his personal office.

BONUS:

Lenin's Mausoleum is an all-red tomb that sits in the middle of the Red Square, and Lenin has chilled inside this thing on display since 1924. When future humanoids dig for our remains, they'll likely think Lenin was our mummy god.

THE GRANDDADDY OF GRAFFITI

Where it all began. The street art in New York City still decorates all of its extremities—from roofs to bodegas to subway tunnels, creeping into tourist photos, and dazzling up advertisements and bar bathrooms. Lace your kicks, look out for the cops, and shake up your paint can—we're throwing up our tag on the NYC graffiti game.

THE BIRTH OF TAGGING

The NYC street art craze began in the late 1960s when a teenage foot-messenger known best as TAKI 183 started to spray his name all across northern Manhattan. Although it's said that another graffiti writer, Julio 204, brought tagging to Manhattan, TAKI 183's fame—including a 1971 *New York Times* cover story—is credited for inspiring others to test their hand at painting up the city's streets.

While some were "getting up" slowly, others "bombed" 'hoods to get their names out there quickly, outfitting Lower East Side tenement buildings in top-to-bottom tags. Bombing hit its heyday in the early '70s and remains popular today.

Moving art installations were created when artists took their talents to the subways. With competition for recognition rising, artists worked at night—alongside giant NYC rats—while tagging subway

cars to move their names throughout the boroughs. Subway cars were wrapped in murals, a large-scale design pioneered by the artist known as Super Kool 223 and mastered by the infamous graffiti quintet, the Fabulous Five.

Just as shit got really interesting, the Clean Train Movement of 1989 decommissioned any train with graffiti on it—leading to poor enough service that the graffiti masters eventually stopped. The MTA is only now realizing how much it pissed off its art-appreciating riders and recently launched various public art promotions— or PG attempts at "cleaning up" graffiti by replacing it with city-approved art. Luckily, regardless of its legality, underground street artists continue to thrive aboveground. Street art in New York continues to grow, spanning vertical space from high up on rooftops to the ground level and down into mole-people territory.

ARTISTS YOU SHOULD KNOW
Known for pioneering a certain style, collaborating on murals, or just covering a lot of city space, in NYC, these artists are essential to the scene:

Tracy 168
Known for creating Wildstyle graffiti by fusing block, bubble, and curling lettering styles.

Fab 5 Freddy
Notorious for merging the hip-hop nation with the graffiti underworld of New York. Although it has long been said that graffiti is simply a visual representation of hip-hop, according to Freddy, both are separate artistic forms of counterculture.

Dr. Revolt
Another old-school artist, the "doctor" painted up subways cars with the best of

them. His mainstream claim to fame was designing the logo for *Yo! MTV Raps*. Word to your mother.

Kenny Scharf
First inspired by Hanna-Barbera cartoons, this Brooklyn artist's signature big-eyed blobs can be found anywhere from East Village mural spaces to the runway, where he collaborated with American designer Jeremy Scott to create a funky-fresh line in 2014. He also got into welding together trash he collected around his Brazil studio and designed a limited-edition wine label for Villa Zapu.

Tats Cru (a.k.a. The Mural Kings)
Muralists (the original three were from the Bronx) who have been painting up large NYC walls and subways for twenty-five years. Artists continue to join the crew every year, painting larger and more elaborate murals, competing in graffiti battles, and even taking part in a documentary to promote their craft. A famous member of the "Cru" was Fat Joe, whose tag name was "Crack."

Cope2
From the South Bronx, Fernando Carlo has been at it since the late '70s, and you can find his bubbled-out name just about anywhere from SoHo billboards to video games to chucks.

FINDING STREET ART

From personal to political, various meaningful pieces cover the city from sewers to delis to bridges to your hostel to our house and back. You're bound to find at least simple tags on any given street block or in any subway station. The popularity of New York street art has even gotten the attention of corporate marketing execs, who place their ads near famous pieces to lure the eyes of art-loving potential consumers. Nonetheless, here are a few places that'll get you in the thick of it:

Train Windows

The best graffiti window-watching can be done from the G train as it emerges aboveground from Brooklyn to Queens (stops: between 21 St.-Jackson Avenue and Court Square).

The Graffiti Hall of Fame

Wrapping an old playground on 106th and Park in East Harlem, this wall has been in a state of artistic evolution for three decades. Home to live graffiti battles, the biggest names in New York street art venture to this famed concrete slab to throw up their pieces.

The Lower East Side

Housing a large concentration of skinny, starving artists, this part of the city contains the legendary graffiti wall near the intersection of Houston and Bowery that has displayed the stylings of various artists for over thirty years. While it's now a fully legal spot to spray, the art that graces its facade changes frequently and is still pretty impressive. Also, you'll be glad to know that the historical tenement buildings are still tagged to shit.

Brooklyn

Catch the L train across the river and go straight into Bushwick. Right off the Jefferson stop, you will be treated to the decorations of Jefftown, organized by a group of street artists called the Bushwick Collective. The group holds special art events but on any given day, the four-block radius around the station is painted up with special pieces by international artists like London's Stik, deconstructionist Nychos, and Brooklyn's most recognizable artist Pixel Pancho.

THE WHOLE ART EXPERIENCE

Paris is really just one big fucking art exhibit. From the world's most trafficked museum to an oil stain on the sidewalk, Parisians have managed to put art everywhere and make everything art. Suffer through the long gallery lines, discover some hidden gems, and soak up the massive street art scene to get the complete art experience.

MUSÉE DU LOUVRE

Why Others Go

A six at best, the "beautiful" *Mona Lisa* is somehow the most famous painting in the world. It has also pretty much been unanimously voted the most overrated tourist attraction in Europe. When you fight through a sea of seniors to view the 30 x 21-inch painting behind a barricade and bulletproof glass, you'll understand why.

Why You Should Go

Luckily, the Louvre redeems itself with 35,000 other pieces that solidify its spot as the best collection in the world. Also, there's enough nakedness here to fill the coffee-table book *Le Louvre Nu* ("The Nude Louvre"), which stars the museum's most beautiful (naked) women. Mona Lisa isn't among them.

Then Hit the Streets

Paris's Belleville neighborhood is the Louvre of street art. Works from every major French street artist is here—including Blek le Rat, JR, Fred le Chevalier, Kouka, Invader, and the 1984 crew. The street art clusterfuck down Rue Dénoyez is the climax, and like any good orgy, it rotates its contributors often.

THE CENTRE POMPIDOU

Why Others Go

Pompidou's National Museum of Modern Art is the second-largest collection of modern and contemporary art in the world, with work from Kandinsky, Picasso, Dalí, and Andy Warhol. Its BPI public library is a favorite among local college students. Like Paris's other art museums, the entrance lines routinely spill onto the street.

Why You Should Go

If you want to avoid the crowd or need to save that 14-euro entrance fee for crêpes, check out the free Atelier Brancusi modern art museum on Pompidou's plaza. Constantin Brancusi was a Romanian sculptor who spent most of his life in Paris. In his will, he left the entire contents of his small Montparnasse studio—from column sculptures to chisels—to the French state on the condition that the studio would be reconstructed *exactly* as it was the day he died. The museum is a glimpse into the creation of his abstract work and his obsession with the spatial relationship of his pieces.

Then Hit the Streets

Even more discreet than the Atelier Brancusi, the subjects of Sandrine Boulet's work are everyday street sites that wouldn't normally catch your attention. Boulet photographs regular objects, then adds illustrations to transform them. An ironing board becomes a butterfly, an excavator becomes a giraffe, an oil stain becomes the hair of Amy Winehouse, and a debris chute and bush become the lower half of a well-endowed Adam and an *au naturale* Eve. Why does Boulet mess with street scenery? Her words: "When you are a kid, you spend hours laying [sic] down in the grass seeing/visualizing amazing things in the clouds. Well, I have decided this should never stop."

MUSÉE D'ORSAY

Why Others Go

In the birthplace of impressionism, Orsay bridges the art movement gap between the Louvre and Pompidou. Plenty of works by Monet, Manet, Renoir, Degas, and Van Gogh make it worth the stop, but with three million visitors a year, the elbow room gets a little tight.

Why You Should Go

The setting, a majestic nineteenth-century train terminal, was almost demolished before being converted into a museum. While tourists funnel through the permanent exhibits, the ever-evolving and always impressive temporary exhibits get much less attention. Orsay also hosts lunchtime concerts, film screenings, and festivals for when you need a little more free movement.

Then Hit the Streets

Princess Hijab, Paris's most reclusive street artist, exhibits her work in train stations in much shorter-term, temporary exhibits. Late at night, Hijab paints black veils over the faces and airbrushed, half-naked bodies of subway fashion advertisements. Her motives could be to draw attention to France's Islamophobic laws against Muslim headdresses or to combat in-your-face sexuality. No one knows who she is, and it's unclear if she really is Muslim or even a female.

PRAGUE'S AA PROGRAM (ABSINTHE AND ARCHITECTURE)

Europe's most elaborate and Grimm-worthy buildings make anyone wonder what the fuck architects were on back in the day. Stop wondering; the answer is absinthe. Often referred to as the "green fairy," absinthe is a vilified but seductive spirit, distilled with wormwood, and is rumored to make you trip hard. Getting lost in the big bad stone woods of Prague's Old Town streets is a must. Might as well bring the fairy along to spice up the ride.

THE TINK OF DRINKS

Up to 180 proof, absinthe is a licorice-flavored green drink traditionally made from hallucinogenic wormwood, anise, and sweet fennel. The first uses of wormwood date back to the ancient Egyptians and Greeks, but it wasn't until the French developed a wine tolerance in the eighteenth century that absinthe grew in popularity. Hallucinogenic fans from Toulouse-Lautrec to Edgar Allan Poe swore that this shit takes it to a new level, though no one has ever proved that the fairy is indeed magical. In a classy joint, it might be served with a sugar cube balanced on a silver spoon, and it's usually diluted with water. The Czechs set theirs on fire and let it simmer down before swallowing. Either way, it's as alcoholic as it gets. Arm yourself with this trip-juice and head to town.

CREEPY OLD TOWN

Prague is divided into ten districts. One of
these, the Old Town, is the epicenter of the
city's cellar-like speakeasies and legendary
electronic clubs. Float till 3:00 a.m. sipping
flaming booze on U Bukanýra, a mutha-
fuckin' houseboat, and then wake up early
to walk it off. Old Town is prime exploring
grounds for lavish buildings, ornate details,
and famous shit. The giant Prague Orloj
(astronomical clock), has been tripping
people out since 1410 on the Old Town
Square. Death, a creepy-as-hell mini skele-
ton, strikes the time, and Apostle figurines
perform an hourly procession. To lighten
up the morbid mood, stare at the swirling
bright pink colors of the Goltz-Kinský
Palace, and then the marble and gold
accents in Malá Strana.

THE PRAGUE CASTLE

On the opposite side of the square is the
Prague Castle, the previous home of royal
families, and currently, the president. The
castle complex has a bunch of exhibition
halls and gardens to wander through.
It's not a castle without a cathedral, and
the Gothic spires of St. Vitus are twisted
enough to start a revolution.

CAFÉ SLAVIA

Once you're good and inspired, visit Prague's go-to hang out for the great romancers of absinthe. The art deco Café Slavia was an idea hub for nineteenth-century Czech visionaries, who drew on the green fairy for artistic inspiration. Instead of adding anise or fennel, the Bohemians drank that shit straight up—made only with wormwood and enough alcohol to fuel an Irish family reunion. When absinthe was "rediscovered" by some Brits in the 1990s, the straight-up stuff got sent out.

HOUSE OF THE BLACK MADONNA

After channeling your inner Van Gogh at Café Slavia, get your Picasso on and stroll by the *House of the Black Madonna* just off Celetná Street in Old Town. Cubist architecture is a Czech thing, so you deserve a flaming shot for the occasion. Once it takes hold, get lost in the intricate jeweled and tiled facades of Josefov (the Jewish quarter). When you're ready to sit down and give your mind a ride, check out an elaborate set at the National Marionette Theater. Puppetry is to Prague what bagels are to New York City.

POP iN FOR A PEEK

At the Futura Gallery in Prague, you can crawl into an asshole using the conveniently built-in stepladder. When you reach the asshole, take a look inside. You will see Czech politicians feeding each other to the song, "We Are The Champions." Controversial artist, David Cerny, built this bold statement, entitled *Brown-nosers*, as a satire of the Czech government. He made it big and gaping so that even people with large heads could pop in for a peek.

ETERNAL GODS OF THE ARTS

For 2,500 years, "The Eternal City" has been pumping out masterpieces in stone and on canvas. From its distinctive ancient architecture during Rome's golden age to the defining sculptures and paintings of the Renaissance, Rome has somehow managed to preserve its art history through centuries of war, earthquakes, and neglect. These are the still-standing highlights from Rome's two greatest eras in this giant museum of a city with a killer food court.

WAY BACK IN THE DAY: ANCIENT ROME

Around 500 BCE, the Roman Forum truly began to take form; it served as the headquarters for all things Roman as the city spent the next millennium rising to and falling from the top of the Western world. The Coliseum is the greatest standing work of Roman architecture and engineering. Back in the day, this is where gladiators slaughtered each other to the delight of the Roman public. The Pantheon is the best-preserved ancient Roman building and was used continuously throughout history as a gathering place for the army, then Catholics, then dead people, and now tourists.

WHEN THINGS GOT REAL ARTSY: RENAISSANCE

The Renaissance, which means "rebirth," marks the period in the fifteenth century when Rome woke up from its 1,000-year-long power nap (otherwise known as the Middle Ages) and decided to regain its awesomeness. Romans rediscovered the works of their golden age, which inspired new movements in literature, science, politics, and most important art. The ceiling of the Sistine Chapel is the masterpiece of all things Renaissance and resides with the pope in the Vatican City.

In violation of the Catholic Church's poverty vow, the Vatican Museums and St. Peter's Basilica hold an art collection worth hundreds of billions of dollars. That popular chapel ceiling, Michelangelo's most famous work, is among the holdings, although he only reluctantly agreed to Pope Julius II's insistence that he create it. In the pope's defense, there is no better way to say "I love Jesus" than intimidating an artist into spending four years painting 5,000 square feet of ceiling teetering a deadly sixty-five feet in the air. Other infamous works here include Raphael's *The School of Athens*, Michelangelo's *Pietà*, Ignazio Danti's *Gallery of Maps*, and Leonardo's *St. Jerome in the Wilderness*.

STILL OLD, NEWER ART: POSTRENAISSANCE

It would have been easy for Rome to call it quits after the Renaissance, sit back with a cannoli, and just marvel at its work, but that wouldn't be very "eternal." A walk around the city will lead you to plenty of more recent gems. The Spanish Steps are great for chilling or working off that gelato. If you throw a coin in the Trevi Fountain, you're guaranteed to return to Rome. Since there's no way you'll tackle all of Rome in one visit (it took the rest of Europe four centuries), that change may be a smart investment.

TATTOO CULTURE

While the Spartans were busy manhandling Xerxes in 300 BCE, the Japanese were inking up. Even before ink, the indigenous Ainu of Japan were marking and scarring themselves with tribal designs to represent honor and beauty. When the Meiji emperor outlawed tattooing in 1868, it was driven underground, and like anything illegal, the more illicit tattooing got, the cooler it became. Nowadays, tattoos are a sacred art form that still makes a rebel statement, and there are more than 500 parlors across Japan.

NEEDLES ALL OVER

Think that back-piece makes you hard? Traditional *irezumi* covers the entire body, shoulder to foot, front to back, with one uninked strip down the middle in the front. A person apprentices for years to become a master tattoo artist of the traditional irezumi style, and once ready, his teacher even gives him a special name: Hori (carved) plus the adopted name of the teacher. The most famous shop in Japan, Scratch Addiction in Tokyo, was the country's first official parlor and is still a pilgrimage site for all serious irezumi enthusiasts. Unique to Japan, this style of tats is only for those serious about pain.

CAN'T MAKE A FULL-BODY COMMITMENT?

The country that gave the world Pokémon and Princess Mononoke has been around the artist block. Men used to hold a monopoly of using or going under the gun, but modern Japanese ladies love their ink. Several top artists in Japan are women, and lady-run Studio Muscat in Tokyo is your best bet for a black and gray. If you're going for color, a dragon symbolizing good luck and wealth is a popular Japanese tattoo. Another good one is a half-sleeve cherry blossom, a Samurai shout-out to honor life's pleasures. If you're an anime nerd looking to represent, hook up with a master geek at Chopstick Tattoo in Osaka.

LOOK BUT DON'T PRICK

The Yokohama Tattoo Museum, run by Horiyoshi III (Japan's unofficial Tattoo King), is a must for any fan of ink culture. It's a small museum dedicated to his personal collection of weird-ass things like shrunken heads and tattooed skulls. Since a tat at the studio upstairs costs as much as a Prius, better give this place a long hard look and take your needle-cravings to the many other shops in the area.

FASHION

We may be filthy, but damn it, we've still got style. Every city around the world has its own fashionable flair, and while the high-end stuff might not squeeze into your budget (or look good crumpled in your backpack), there are thrifty ways to stay on top of the fashion pulse no matter where you find yourself. Whether you're sporting bright colors for Diwali, secondhand store-hopping in NYC, or haggling down the price of leather overalls in Italy, all you need to look good abroad is a little creativity and confidence (and perhaps a hot shower).

HK IN HK—HELLO KITTY FASHIONS

With over 20,000 official HK products on the market, and Hello Kitty–themed fucking everything, this cat has her claws deep into the hearts (and pockets) of all of Asia, especially Hong Kong—where she has held office as the Official Ambassador of Tourism since 2008.

BIG KITTY STYLES

While fashion trends come and go, in Hong Kong the kitty is always in style. On the streets, you will find a colorful array of feline fashions. HK's face is printed on absolutely everything: shoes, shirts, bags, and coats, often in loud and clashing combined outfits dedicated to nothing but cat. Raining out? Grab your trusty HK umbrella to keep your HK raincoat dry. What time is it? According to your HK wristwatch, it's always Hello Kitty o'clock.

KITTY CULTURE

Born in Japan, Kitty White—street name: Hello Kitty—said *konnichiwa* for the first time in 1974. Sometime before Miss White's feline face hawked its first product (a coin purse), the Japanese began adopting the *kawaii* ("cute" or "adorable") culture—spawning a phenomenon of happy-good-fun-lucky times on everything from key chains to couture. The Japanese company Sanrio hopped on the cute train when Yuko Shimizu, an in-house designer, drew a white, Japanese bobtail cat with a big red bow and no mouth. Sanrio wanted to keep their signature kitty mute so that people "could project their [own] feelings onto the character." Our feeling is that this cat will give it up to anyone (Nike, Vans, Kimmora Lee Simmons, Swarovski, Stüssy, Fender) who's willing to pay to play with her.

GOOD KITTY

What is it about this pasty cat with a big-ass head that people go meowzers over? The ultimate example of "right time, right place." People asked for cute, Sanrio gave them a cat without a mouth. And although she may not say much, this doesn't seem to stop freakish followers from buying just about anything with Hello Kitty's face on it. Stop by the Hello Kitty store in Hong Kong and pick up your very own Hello Kitty ice cream churner, humidifier, bedazzled hoodie, or hot-dog maker! And next time you think about tying the knot, consider booking the Hong Kong subway station and riding the "Hello Kitty Wedding Train" like one couple did in 2007—the bride was dazzling in her Hello Kitty wedding dress, which matched her Hello Kitty engagement ring *purr*fectly.

BAD KITTY

If the 20,000 official Hello Kitty products aren't enough, perhaps you could browse through the millions of *un*official products, like the Hello Kitty ball-gag or Hello Kitty latex bed. Pick up a bottle of Hello Kitty Pink Grey Goose Vodka or a sixer of Hello Kitty Beck's. And nothing screams *kawaii*, peace, and love like the custom Hello Kitty AK-47.

Even though this kitty has no mouth, we're convinced she is laughing all the way to the bank. With a stronghold on the street fashions of Hong Kong, Ms. Kitty is reaping over $5 billion each year, and there's no sign that anyone will sour of this old puss anytime soon.

PUSSY PILOT

Taiwanese EVA Air can fly you into Hong Kong in proper Hello Kitty style. Each plane in their limited Asian route is decorated in one of five themes: Hello Kitty Happy Music Time, Hello Kitty Loves Apples, Hello Kitty with Magic Stars, Hello Kitty Around the World, and Hello Kitty Speed Puff. From the giant pink HK kiosks to a silhouette of the feline's face on every food item served on board (kitty cantaloupe, anyone?)—every detail is the cat's meow.

INDIA

HOW TO DRESS FOR DIWALI

This autumn festival of lights is all about good conquering evil—but wearing your Halloween Batman cape isn't going to cut it. Celebrated from India to Fiji, parts of Africa to France, Australia to Sri Lanka, this holiday is about looking good, eating well, and starting again. Diwali is a special time where old is turned into new, and sporting your newest, freshest threads is how you dress to impress.

HIN-DO IT RIGHT

Both a harvest festival and the marking of a new year, Diwali—also called the "festival of lights" and Deepavali—is celebrated differently by several religious groups including Sikhs, Buddhists, Jains, and Hindus. While it varies regionally as well, Hindus pray primarily to Lakshmi—the goddess of prosperity and wealth—and stretch the whole shebang out for five days.

People celebrate by indulging in *mithai* (traditional sweets) and blast colorful fireworks into the night sky.

=== *Fun Fact* ===

Since Diwali is ultimately a festival of peace, every year, troops on the Indian and Pakistani border share sweets.

SHOP 'TILL YOU DROP

The biggest shopping day of the year, Diwali is like Black Friday; people scramble to buy fresh new outfits and gifts for family during the holiday season. Stores are flooded with shoppers looking for the coolest sarees, gold and silver jewelry, and housewares. While you won't be fighting over a Tickle Me Elmo like you might in your Black Friday rage, you might consider buying a bunch of firecrackers, as India uses about $800 million of them each year during Diwali. As far as fashion goes, wearing drab black or gray won't cut it here; the festival is all about lights and holiday brights.

STYLE TIPS

Soiree Sarees

The *saree* (a.k.a. sari), or the draped dress Western folk typically associate with Indian formal wear, isn't the only soiree style. A variation of the traditional *salwar kameez*, an *anarkali* is an outfit that consists of a long dress-like top, sometimes slim pants underneath of the same color, and a matching *dupatta* (scarf). To show more skin, a *lehenga* is a long pleated skirt many wear with *choli* (crop tops) that let you show off those belly-dancing abs in style.

Bejeweled

Diwali isn't the time to hold back on adornments. Even if your outfit is already killin' it in the color and embellishment department, there's always room for jewelry. Traditional items include earrings such as *jhumkas* (bell-shaped) or *chaand balis* (ornate hoops), or many bracelets (called bangles or *kadas*). If you have a nose hoop, connecting it to your ear with a chain is a festive look.

Fab Feet

Don't you dare get caught with Chucks peeking out from those gorgeous layers of fabric. Diwali footwear isn't standardized but strappy metallic sandals or simple flats are a nice accent.

Menswear

Men start with a *kurta*, or a long collarless fancy shirt that'll fall somewhere around your knees. Kurtas can be a solid color, but wildly embellished is the way to go for Diwali. Shorter kurtas (which are really just shirts) are available if you're not quite ready for a man dress. As far as bottoms are concerned, you've got options: *Churidaar* are slim-bottomed pants worn by men and women, and if your junk needs a breather, wrap-around *dhoti* are the way to go. Even though some people think it's okay to wear jeans under all the fabric and adornment, save your denim for another day and get down with this fashionably fun tradition instead.

COUNTERFEIT IT—A GUIDE TO KNOCKOFF SHOPPING

It's estimated that 10 percent of all designer goods in Italy are big ol' fakers. The demand for Pucci, Gucci, and other high-end Italian brands that don't end in "ucci" are as fierce as the price tags of these coveted items. Don't be fooled by the seemingly fancy getups of high-strutting Italians; knockoffs can be bought everywhere, and even though no Italian would admit to wearing fake Prada, check the label next time you get a local to drop their pants.

PAYING THE PRICE

Before you start hagglin' for a fake Fendi backpack to fill with knockoff goods that are "Made in Italy," consider the pricey consequences for buying counterfeits: a fine of up to 10,000 euros. In an attempt to drastically reduce the demand for rip-off label whoring, the Italian authorities are holding the shopper accountable—even the "unsuspecting" tourist, unaware of the law, could end up coughing up 10,000 euros for Prada's pleather cousin.

GOODIES ON-THE-GO

If you are willing to risk the fines for a fake, you don't have to look very hard or spend an Armani-and-a-leg to find one. When in Rome, head toward the area near the Spanish Steps—the equivalent of New York's Fifth Avenue or Paris's Champs-Élysées—to gawk at the real deals, then look for the guys peddlin' on the pavement with big, black duffel bags full of more affordable options. In need of some free afternoon entertainment? Hang around and wait for the *polizia* to roll through—the makeshift shops for fakes turn mobile in an instant as the "shop owners" flee the authorities. Florence and Milan host the same scene.

Look for a crowd of tourists surrounding goods on the ground—then look right and left for coppers before buying.

LABEL-LESS LEATHERS

If you couldn't give less of a shit about labels, then your options for bagging quality Italian goods—like leather—without risking run-ins with the law significantly increase. Bring home a real souvenir made of Italian leather by sifting through the skins in Florence, the leather capital of Italy. The Santa Croce Leather Workshop, located in the cloister of the Santa Croce Church, is the leathery mecca, but also take a look-see at the San Lorenzo Market, where bringing your bargaining game face is essential. Wandering off the beaten path of any market can host perfect "leather-weather"—head down the side streets of smaller villages for a personal experience with artisans and a chance to score more for less.

Whether riskin' a bad rap for a good price or ditching the label and paying less, there is no shortage of deals to be found on Italy's fashionable streets. No matter what the label on your bag says, it should never read *full price*.

HAGGLING LIKE AN INTERNATIONAL BOSS

Vendors everywhere are like hungry hawks, and a shopping tourist is their wounded prey. They'll be watching you from the moment you enter the market, sniffing for weakness. So, put on your best scowl, get focused, and stay sharp. Keep these tips tucked in your pocket to score big discounts on random shit at the market:

1. Know how much you are willing to spend before entering the playing field, and don't be afraid to walk away.

2. Face it: no one's buying that you're a local, but knowing a few key phrases in the local language will open the cheap shopping floodgates.

3. Haggling is like dating. You have to romance the vendor a little before you get the goods. Wink, smile, and nod as you talk up his treasure, then "psshhh!" at what he says it costs.

4. Offer the vendor half the asking price *minus one*. Since half is the expected counterwager, going one lower shows that you know the game and mean business. He'll either be impressed by your showmanship or think you're a jerk-off.

5. A skilled vendor will tug at your heartstrings or fuck with your head to gain access to your wallet. Stick to your plan regardless of whether his fifteen daughters need braces. Even if your new vendor buddy puts his arm around your shoulder, serves you tea, and tells you stories he's never told *anyone*, you don't owe him shit.

6. If you find yourself agreeing with him when you initially didn't, take a step away for some fresh air. Chances are whatever you want will still be there once you return, this time with ice running through your veins.

7. When it comes to haggling, sometimes lying is the best policy. "The guy down the block o'er there has this same exact thing for three bucks cheaper. Should I just go buy it from him?"

8. Buying in bulk adds leverage. If you have extra room in your pack, the two-for-one haggling trick can get you what you want, plus another something you may not want.

Once you're both winded from the bargaining boogie, the final step is to look the vendor straight in the eye, lay down your final offer, and shut the fuck up. Let it linger like a silent-but-deadly fart. Stand there and bask in the stench, until he either gives in to your offer, or you cave and buy the damn elephant statue for thirty cents more.

WORLD COSPLAY SUMMIT

Japan plays dress-up on a whole different level. This isn't some shitty sheet you try to pass off as a ghost; a lot more work goes into transforming into your favorite character. Being part of the mother of cosplay events is going to require some major nerd dedication; a shit ton of body paint, tutus, and glitter; and costuming creativity. Step into the world of arguably the most serious hobby on the planet.

CRAY CRAY ANIME

The summit takes place every year in Nagoya, Japan and draws cosplayers from around the world who construct elaborate costumes and sets, with plenty of schoolgirl outfits and obscure monster villains. The term "cosplay" (costume play) was actually coined there. The summit started in 2003 with a small but dedicated following.

Nowadays, the WCS is held at the Aichi Arts Center—the largest venue in town—and teams from about thirty countries compete. People spend an entire year building their costumes from scratch in their respective countries and competing at preliminary cons, all for the chance to show off their craftiness at this event every year.

OFFICIAL RULES

Entry is limited to pairs of players, and you must have citizenship in the country you are representing. You must bring three costumes—one each for the parade, championship, and "courtesy visits"—to Japan. You may not wear a Mickey Mouse outfit or some weird Trekkie shit; the costume must originate from Japanese anime, manga, tokusatsu, and video games. All costumes and props (like swords) must be handmade; anything from a bag will get you the boot. Once onstage, you have two minutes and thirty seconds to "perform," whatever that means to you. Judging happens in two parts: onstage performance and the craftsmanship of your getup. Judges not only look for how well you embody the characters you represent but also how neatly you stitch and paint your costume and props. What's at stake? Global geek fame!

QUALCONS

If you get crafty, you can con your way into a free ticket to Japan. Cons are held around the world as qualifiers for that country to send their best-dressed to Japan. The winners of local competitions are awarded cash prizes to be used toward bettering their costumes and sometimes (listen up!) free flights to Japan. Gather all your glitz and glue and hit up the three largest anime cons in the US, held in Los Angeles, Baltimore, and Chicago.

NEW YORK CITY

SECONDHAND CLOTHES THAT DON'T SMELL LIKE MOTHBALLS

Fashion rules New York. The streets are like runways with style oozing from every corner. What's that? You didn't pack the new Dolce & Gabbana spring line into your backpack? Fear not. Although famous Fifth Avenue is lined with stores even your sugar daddy (or mama) couldn't afford, there are several low-budget options when it comes to shopping for threads. As important as fashion is here, creativity takes precedence (and that's free). So use the streets for inspiration and find creative, cheaper alternatives at the places below.

BUFFALO EXCHANGE AND BEACON'S CLOSET

These are two chains that work in similar ways. Both are combo stores of both new and secondhand clothes and accessories, with several stores in Brooklyn and Manhattan. The stores are well organized and have sections for both girls and guys. Basically, sellers bring in their gently used, recently fashionable clothes; then a skilled store clerk sorts through their stuff (some of which is expensive designer gear that the seller outgrew horizontally) and picks items they feel will sell best in the store. The seller can then choose to get either store credit or cash for the items the store takes.

What this all means to you, especially in New York, is that you get to scavenge through nice, almost new, fashionable things and pay very little for your finds. Additionally, the items you find reflect the neighborhood in which they're sold, so you really get a sense of the local fashion preferences.

CENTURY 21

A retailer of discounted designer clothing, shoes, and accessories, their motto is "fashion worth fighting for." If buying big name brands without the high price tags is your thing, this is the place to go. The styles are often for older people (say, midlife-crisis time), but you can find a good deal if you look hard. This place is huge, so you will get your fashion fight on—for hours.

GOODWILL/SALVATION ARMY

There is nothing shameful about shopping at Goodwill. Though people used to equate these stores with soup kitchens, these places have seen a resurrection with the fashionable budget shopper. Sure these stores are full of some pretty useless junk (VCRs and Walkmans circa 1993), but lots of fashionable New Yorkers donate their sassy stuff to these places for tax write-offs, so it may be worth the dig.

The trick to keeping up with New York style on a budget is steering away from the conventional and shopping at places that require a little more browsing. After all, in this fashionable city, one man's trash is probably much more fashionable than your own trash.

DRESSED TO KILL

If you thought loveable little guinea pigs couldn't get any cuter, the town of Huacho, Peru, has taken their preciousness to a new level. In the annual Festival of the Guinea Pig, our snugalicious pets are dressed in darling outfits to look like furry, pint-size people and compete for the titles of absofucklinglute adorability. Over in the food stalls however, some of their less fortunate colleagues are fried whole and served with rice and veggies. Guinea pigs star in every part of the festival—from the main stage to the main course.

BEFORE YOU JUDGE . . .

Long before Mr. Fluff Monster was your kindergarten classroom pet, guinea pigs were domesticated by the Andean people for their meat, not their cuddliness. Called *cuy* (pronounced "kwee") in Spanish and rarely, but more accurately, *cavy* (pronounced "KAY-vee") in English, they bang like bunnies and taste (almost) like chicken. These cheap, low-maintenance rodents grow up fast and are lean in fat and high in protein. In rural Andean homes, you'll find dozens of cuy frolicking and fornicating at will—until someone gets hungry. They are not pets, nor pigs, nor from Guinea . . . so we pretty much got it completely wrong.

THE FASHION SHOW

Villages throughout Ecuador, Peru, and Bolivia throw annual fiestas to honor these rats with better PR. In Huacho, the cuy catwalk takes center stage. Many are dressed in traditional outfits, often to match their owners. Others are dressed as kings, nobles, farmers, peasants, miners, folk singers, and even Santa Claus. Prizes are dished out for the best-dressed cuy, along with the fattest, fastest, and, of course, tastiest. You won't find an official website about this July festival, so brush up your Español, fly down to Lima, catch a bus up the coast to Huacho, and ask around. Pack a tiny trumpet and bow tie for Cuy Armstrong, a mini coonskin cap for Cavy Crockett, and some hair grease and a secondhand suit for My Cousin Guinea. You could be the first gringo winner—or even participant—the festival has ever seen. And you probably already know what's served at the victory dinner.

WEST AFRICA

SERIOUS FASHION

Like the region itself, West African fashion is often misrepresented. Stereotyped as a place that is too poor to care about fashion or too exotic to be relevant, West Africa doesn't just offer animal print threads and crazy tribal neck gear. On the contrary, the region is pumping out some serious fashion that's quickly creepin' onto every major, modern runway from New York to Milan.

FABRIC OF WEST AFRICAN FASHION

Traditional textiles, as bold and original as the region and its history, are setting trends on every continent. Those sweet, colorful, geometric leggings you scored at Urban Outfitters? They were probably inspired by Ghanaian *kente* cloth. When the Akan people of Ghana and the Ivory Coast first introduced the most famous of all African fabrics, it was considered a fabric fit only for a king.

Nowadays, kente-style cloth is fitting just about every class of hot ass around the globe. Those boldly patterned, batik-style fabrics that are being turned into designer booty-shorts for Beyoncé or a one-of-a-kind jacket for Lady Gaga—every designer from Marc Jacobs to Tory Burch can thank West African Ankara fabric for influencing their

designs. And although the *ankara*-style was a result of Dutch-colonial influence, West Africans immediately spun their creativity and cultural heritage into every fiber of the signature cloth.

STRIKING A POSE

Unlike many of the Western fashion trends that are dictated by massive marketing campaigns, West African fashion celebrates creativity, originality, and the importance of personal style. Many West Africans choose to entertain their inner Armani by picking a fabric they connect with and commissioning a seamstress to make the garment just the way they want. Talented designers are emerging from this scene, like Nigerian Lisa Folawiyo, founder of world-renowned brand Jewel by Lisa. Her ever-evolving lines celebrate the deep cultural and social significance of traditional fabrics in their designs—with an added personal touch, like Swarovski crystal embroidering. Judging by the hordes of Western world copycats, West Africa has become a big fucking fashion deal.

NAME-DROPPIN'

Maybe Deola Sagoe is not a household name like Coco Chanel, but this Nigerian designer has peeps like Oprah and Will Smith begging for her haute couture that has been featured in many a Fashion Week.

Expect to hear more about Loza Maléombho, an innovative designer raised in Ivory Coast and based out of New York City. This edgy designer is using fashion not only to raise awareness of West African heritage, but also as a tool for the social empowerment of West African women. She employs local women from Ivory Coast, pays them fair wages, teaches them how to manage money, and showcases their talents on the global runway.

Although the region is still shrouded in images of *National Geographic* loin cloths, West Africa is combining its dynamic history and modern artistry to produce unique, street-ready fashion.

MAKING CASH OUT OF TRASH

Making use of imported Western garbage, like plastic and glass bottles, West Africans have found numerous ways to turn junk into jingles. Ghana takes the bead lead by recycling bottles, broken windshields, and any other shattered glass to make Krobo beads. In Burkina Faso, plastic prayer mats are recycled into colorful bracelets. Bronze jewelry turns green these days in Mali, where abandoned bronze radiators are pounded out and transformed into earrings.

FOOD

World cuisine is best eaten from a street cart. Seek out traditional dishes, avoid the familiar arches and java, and don't be afraid to wrap your taste buds around the absurd. In our most delicious chapter, you'll learn how to get down with crêpes in iconic France, Burmese salads, and pizza in Italy. We threw a few chicken fetuses (Vietnam), sheep's heads (Iceland), and fried ants (Chiapas, Mexico) into the mix as a crunchy top layer of food exploration fun. Your stomach may be angry with you when all is said and eaten, but sampling authentic local food is a great way to dive into local culture, mouth-first.

BURMA LOVE

Burma (also known as Myanmar) is home to an array of dishes influenced by surrounding cuisines. Where the rest of the world just dresses their salad with vinegar, oil, or a creamy concoction of some sort, Burma throws on fermented tea leaves and lemon to create a tasty adventure like no other. A combo of flavors, Burmese food is kind of like Indian food with Asian preparations, and it will make your mouth feel the love in this eclectic country.

DOSA

These pancakes should be familiar to you if you've ever indulged in Indian cuisines. Dosas here are called "kauk mote" or "folded snacks." In Yangon—the former capital and the nation's largest city—dosas are the most popular street side snack and come in both savory and sweet varieties. On the savory spectrum, you can get the Indian flavors you're used to (filled with potatoes and served with chutneys) or go for a more real-Burmese deal with shredded carrots and cabbage, bean sprouts, beans, and tomatoes. On the sweet side, dosas here are also filled with palm sugar and shredded coconut.

SALADS

Salads are salads, unless you are in Burma, where salad takes on a whole new flavor that'll shock your taste buds into submission. Burma is known for turning a seemingly bland romaine-based salad into something spectacular with a fermented black tea dressing, a handful of crunchy additions like fried garlic and dried shrimp, crunchy beans, and a generous spritz of lemon. Along with the popular tea leaf salad, many noodle-based and fish-sauce spiced salad varieties exist in Burma. It makes zero sense for these salads to taste good but holy shit, they'll put a spell on you.

FISH

Burma doesn't fuck with fillets! These people grill that sucker whole and spice it up so nice it'll make you want to have dinner twice. Called nga kin, the traditional recipe for whole grilled fish calls for a

whole fish stuffed with a mixture of herbs, chilies, and salt, which is then charred and served with a tamarind dipping sauce. Beer is the drink of choice here and pairing local brews with a whole fish is the ticket to Burmese paradise.

OTP Tip: Mohinga is a staple which consists of rice noodles swimming in fish stew and topped with crispy fried onions. Sound like a good lunch or dinner? Well, too bad, because this national dish is consumed for breakfast. Step up to fish in the morning like a champion.

SKEWERS

Burma loves to stick sticks into chunks of food, from veggies to pork, and fire it up on the barbie. Here, nothing is off-limits. Skewered pig livers, lungs, intestines, ears, and testicles are up for grabs and are often served street-side with hot soup and dipping sauce (made of chili, tomato, and ginger).

CURRY

We won't hesitate to claim that everyone loves curry. Burma's version lacks the coconut milk most Southeast Asian curries feature and instead utilizes fresh onion for body, a whole lot of oil, and a fermented fish paste (called *ngapi*) that gives the curry an umami flavor.

SWEETS

Dessert here is heavy on the jellies, dense cakes, and fruit, particularly bananas. Popular sweets include a funnel cake–like concoction called *gyalebi*, *kauknyintok* (banana steamed in banana leaf with coconut cream and sesame seeds), *hpa luda* (a parfait featuring rose water, milk, jello, and coconut shavings), and *mote lone yay paw* (or "teething cake") a floury sweet prepared in celebration of a baby's first tooth.

OTP Tip: *Jaggery* are sugar chunks that have a maple-like flavor and are excellent in tea.

NOT A TACO BELL IN SIGHT

Way more than the bastardized burritos and nachos you pick up at window #2, Mexican food is such a big deal, the cuisine was named by UNESCO as an intangible cultural heritage of mankind. Spicy, tangy, and full of rich soul, the Chiapas region is also the cheapest in all of Mexico, making all its edibles available to you at street-food prices.

ELOTE

In Chiapas, it all starts with corn, a sacred crop deeply embedded in Mayan culture and considered a gift from the gods. *Elote* (corn on the cob) is a major street food and is usually grilled, then superslathered in mayo. To layer flavor on your natural stick of Mexican food history, other topping options include chile powder, butter, salt, grated cotija cheese, salsa picante, and lemon or lime juice. If picking corn out of your teeth on the streets gets grueling, check out elote's loose cousin, e*squites*, an off-the-cob version served in a bowl with a mixture of the above ingredients and eaten with a spoon.

OTP Tip: Add some corn to your corn by chugging down *pozol*, a drink made of corn dough and water (*pozol blanco*), or mixed with cacao (*pozol de cacao*), and popular during Mayan ceremonies where it was believed to help the indígenas make long journeys through the jungle. When your corn baby fully matures, flush and don't look down.

NUCÚ

Why yes, those are curled up ant legs on your plate. A Chiapas specialty, *nucú* (a.k.a. *chicatana*) are essentially oversize queen ants filled with thousands of eggs. They're usually roasted and salted, served with lime juice and chile powder, and sometimes sprinkled on tacos (if you like an extra crunch). Nucú mate in swarm-orgies every June, after which all the males die, leaving bloated females to sit around until dinnertime. Best to take off their head and direct your bite straight at their fat asses.

LENGUA

If your own tongue just ain't cutting it anymore, *lengua* is your mouth's chance to get real personal with beef tongue. Rubbing taste buds with a cow may sound like twisted bestiality, but the meat is chewy, with a dense, smooth texture and a not-half-bad taste. You can find a lickin' in burritos and tacos, or on its own with a sauce. Try it with saffron sauce (*lengua en salsa de azafran*) to make you, and your new beefy friend, salivate.

TACOS

Instead of giving you our gringo taco banter, while in Chiapas, OTP was lucky enough to meet Jesús Catalán, the self-proclaimed "Taco King," and he's better equipped to give you the deep insider view of Mexico's favorite sandwich. Catalán is legit: Born in Del Valle, the taco epicenter of Mexico City, he has consumed millions of tacos around the world and, after seventeen years, still holds the record for eating the most street-style *tacos de canasta* (sixty-three of those bad boys!) in a single sitting.

So, what makes a good taco? Catalán says it's all about "tortillas, beans, chile, the fresh ingredients of a salsa, and the essential squeeze of lime." He's willing to get on an airplane for his Chiapan taco fix. At *puestos* (DIY taco joints) at the shore of Lago Pojol in El Parque Nacional Lagunas de Montebello, ". . . you'll find homemade fresh cheese wrapped in banana leaves, that will be grilled and topped with black beans, fried chorizo, and avocado slices. Ask for tortillas and make tacos, those are really authentic." Catalán swears that, "God is a taquero, life is a puesto, love is the salsa, and you are the taco." To Catalán, tacos in Chiapas are a big deal, and he's ready to wage war on anyone trying to mess with his favorite street eats. In fact, he ". . . dare[s] anyone with a passion for tacos to bring it on and try to steal [his] crown." You hear that? *Be* the taco.

TAMALES

These are not your freezer section logs of awful. Chiapas' nutty version, called *tamales chiapanecos*, are a regional creation. They come wrapped in banana leaves and filled with pork, raisins, tomatoes, almonds, onions, and spicy herbs. The dough contains *chipilín*, an herb native to Chiapas that gives these tamales a little extra flair. Purchase yours from any guy peddling them from his bike.

Superagriculturalists since before America was "born," you best believe the people of Chiapas know their shit when it comes to food. The Taco King will tell you: "In such a diverse country as Mexico, food is perhaps the strongest element that 'glues' us all. Old and young, rich and poor, religious or not." Combine that with the "mi casa es su casa" mentality of the region, and you got yourself a street feast worth a trip way south of the border.

TACO KING SAYS . . .

"Always look for the crowd, which not only indicates deliciousness and hygiene, but also a good price. Ask for tacos 'con copia,' which means two tortillas instead of just one per taco."

CRÊPE YOUR PANTS

French food gives us a *boner appétit*. From their locally grown food picked fresh from their diverse landscapes, to their willingness to eat anything and everything, the French are true chefs who make everyone else look like lowly line cooks. Even back in the Middle Ages, when royalty from neighboring countries wanted a special feast, they ordered out from France, in what was probably the slowest delivery service ever. Crêpes are the centerpiece of French cuisine and can be eaten anywhere, at any time, and on any budget.

THE SKINNY ON CRÊPES

Crêpes are pretty simple—pour a thin layer of batter on a skillet and cook until it's like a giant, ultrathin pancake. Then throw whatever ingredients you want on top and wrap it up.

SWEET CRÊPES

Superthin, white sheets of lightly sweetened wheat flour are stuffed with fruit, jam, or any sort of sugary filling or spread. Nutella—a hazelnut spread that, in the rest of the world, has made peanut butter its bitch—is a favorite. Go sweet for breakfast, dessert, or some post-toke munchies.

NATIONAL CRÊPE DAY

February 2 is National Crêpe Day! It is said that if, on this day, you can catch a crêpe with a frying pan after tossing it in the air with your right hand while holding a gold coin in your left, you will become rich that year. Before you start making any judgments about this tradition, remember that on that same day each year, you watch with bated breath as a rodent predicts the global climate for the next six weeks. We'd rather eat crêpes.

SAVORY GALETTES

A "dark meat" variation, galettes are made with unsweetened, darker buckwheat batter and filled with anything from veggies and cheese to beef burgundy for a cheap lunch or dinner. Smelly French cheese melted all over earthy mushrooms is a great way to go.

ALL CRÊPE-D OUT

Throw ice cream on it, and you have *crêpe à la mode*. Set Grand Marnier on fire, pour it on top, and you have *crêpe suzette*. Roll it up like a cigar, bake it, and have it with afternoon tea for *crêpe dentelle*. Stack a dozen crêpes on top of one another with filling in between each, and you have a *mille crêpe* cake. And in traditional French fashion, be sure you wash it all down with some alcoholic cider.

CREEP UP ON CRÊPES

Crêpes are the food of choice for poor Parisians, so *crêperies* are as prevalent as topless ladies on a French beach. Find them near the starving artists in Montmartre and broke college students in the Latin Quarter. The best spot to get crêpes, though, is their birthplace in Brittany, France. When crêpe chefs from that area traveled to Paris, they set up shop just outside the Montparnasse train station, where they still whip up the best crêpes in town.

VEGGIN' OUT

While the term "hamburger" was born here, eating zero meat in Germany's second-largest city isn't as hard as you'd think. Despite its sausage-filled food history, Germany is trending toward plants, and whether you're hanging with a beer street-side, sipping a brew at a restaurant, or chugging it down with your Airbnb host, finding complementary food is a piece of vegan (German Chocolate) cake.

STREET-SIDE

You want your all vegan food truck with a little *Men in Black* flare? Meet Vincent Vegan, or vegan badassery on wheels. This mobile vegan food dispensary serves up currywurst, cheesy beef burgers (made with seitan and tofu), and fries (regular or sweet) with dips like redchup, vayonaise, and (super popular) garlicky turmeric. The truck started as a passion project in 2014 that brought together a collective of fourteen members from different walks of life. If it's greasy (but not animal fat-laden) comfort food you're after, Vincent's got the street-side hook up.

SAVOR

For sit-down options, the Vegan Eagle is ground zero. They have your veggie burgers and bowls of whatever veg, but take it up a notch with curries, bean-packed chili, and desserts like apple crumbles and brownies. Plus beer—so much beer. The Leaf—with an ambiance created by creaky wooden tables and bright windows—is also a local favorite that serves traditional (but veganized) German fare plus international dishes like Indian pistachio coconut milk rice and meatballs and lasagna with braised radicchio. If you've piggy-banked some euros, spend them at Aloha Cherie, a Mediterranean-inspired German fusion joint with perfect sunny-day outdoor seating.

SIP

Almond milk in your coffee and vegan pastries on display, Hamburg's got you covered when it comes to your caffeinating needs. Cafés around town sport the latest in vegan fare, including nut milk options, full-on vegan brunches, and cakes that leave out the dairy without compromising on flavor. Kaffeeklappe is an out-of-the-way café in Elbe that has your coffee, cake, quirk, and dirt-cheap vegan breakfast.

=== *Fun Fact* ===

The owners are not named Vincent; so who the fuck is Vincent then? According to the owners, "Vincent Vegan is a rebel, a very smooth rebel. Vincent represents the light side of the Force. Vincent is a vegan Jedi and Agent Zero for the veggie secret service. Vincent's mission is clear: to advance uncompromisingly, with love in our hearts and a fire in our souls. The attack on conventional food has only just begun."

SAUSAGE BREAKDOWN

If the only vegetable you'll ever eat is a sausage, Germany's got you covered with several native varieties. Here are the five best of the wurst:

Knackwurst
The baby of the bunch, these snappy-skinned chubbies are made from pork and pungent ground garlic and taste great with a good 'kraut.

Bockwurst
A firm sausage made with veal, pork, cream, and eggs, and spiced with parsley, this one goes down best with a Bock beer—although we wouldn't be mad if you had a dab of delicious mustard instead.

Wollwurst
This guy just lets it all hang out! You won't find an inch of casing pinching the supple pork and veal composition of this wurst; just a smooth meat tube that's first boiled, then fried so that's it's smooth on the inside and crispy outside.

Weisswurst
The fair-skinned Belgian sister, this sausage is boiled and is a blander take on meat—in this case veal—mashed together.

Landjäger
A super savory, hard salami-like sausage stick that's as good on a plate as it is in your pocket when you need a meaty pick-me-up.

Blood Bonus: Blutwurst
A blood sausage typically made from pig's blood, pork, and seasonings, all rolled up in an intestine and served black and coagulated.

OTP Tip: *Kumpir* (baked potatoes) are a common street food that can easily be veganized if you ask for no *kase* (cheese) or *sauerrahm* (sour cream).

SHOP
With nine locations across Europe, Veganz is an all-vegan supermarket that first opened its doors to vegheads in 2011 and carries 6,000 vegan products from 200 international suppliers. While you'll find a bunch of amazing grocery stores around town, Veganz is top-notch when you're looking for nothing but vegan groceries. Here, you'll find strange meat and dairy alternatives, but also raw desserts, a dedicated bistro, and a cantina serving juice, smoothies, and coffee. Additionally, markets like Alnatura, Kaufmannslauden, and denn's Biomarkt are great suppliers of good vegan goods.

OTP Tip: If you fall in love with Veganz, you can literally date the market as it offers movie nights, cooking classes, and frequent workshops.

SURF AND TURF WITH WINGS

The lobster, steak, and chicken platter in Iceland is a little different. Their "surf" is bigger, their "turf" is badder, and their "wings" are international icons. Living in a fairly remote island nation, Icelanders have historically eaten some weird-ass shit to sustain themselves. Here are three pickings to shock your palette.

SURF

Whale: The Other Red Meat

A beached whale is normally a sad scene. You think about *Free Willy* and wonder how the world can be so cruel, tossing this majestic being out of its waters to perish on the hot shore. While you play out the sob story in your head, Icelanders come a runnin' with forks and knives. The Minke whale is popular in Icelandic cuisine and, while it's

usually served grilled or on a skewer, can be fancied-up and eaten sashimi-style.

FERMENTED BOOZE: BRENNIVÍN

How could you go wrong with a drink known as Black Death? Brennivín, which appropriately translates to "burning wine," is the signature drink in Iceland. This concoction of fermented potato mash with caraway seeds, cumin, and angelica tastes like rye bread soaked in gasoline. You won't find an Icelander with an income drinking it, so who does? Budd from *Kill Bill*, David Grohl in a song where he's turning to "Skin and Bones," and Icelandic good-for-nothing drunks and others with similar finances and hygiene (a.k.a. *you*).

TURF

Deep in Sheep

Forget your chef's knife; to prepare svið, you'll need a saw. This traditional Icelandic dish is prepared by first singeing off all remaining fur on a sheep's head, sawing it in half through the brains and down the jaw, then tossing the sucker with some salt, and throwing it in a pot to slow simmer. All kinds of interesting superstitions exist around eating the various parts of the head. For instance, if the bone found under the tongue stays intact, a local baby will never learn to speak. The eyeballs are said to be finger-lickin' good. Normally served with much tamer sides (like mashed potatoes), this turf fare is available at both cheap eats and high-end restaurants.

WINGS

Puffins

Gracing the covers of cereal boxes everywhere, chubby, penguin-like puffins are native to Iceland. You may have crunched down on their carb-y breakfast products, but Icelanders used to eat the real deal until the lovable bird population steeply declined. You may find some off-the-books puffin dishes flapping around the outskirts of the island, but for the most part, these birds are now reserved for picture-taking and not devouring.

PAGAN FOOD FEST

Þorrablót (or *Thurseblot*, in case you're not one of the eleven or so people who speak Icelandic) is a festival held in mid-January, when the locals get sick of being bitch-slapped by the frost. Dedicated to Thor, a Norse god associated with everything that's stormy and terrible, this food-focused celebration begs him to hammer back the winter and let the spring warm the island. The first day of Thurseblot is called *Bóndadagur*, or "Husband's Day," and traditionally, women bring the men breakfast in bed–just as the men will do on *Konudagur*, "Woman's Day" (if they know what's good for them).

Most Icelanders celebrate Thurseblot at home with friends, but you can find some restaurants serving traditional foods as well. Far from pumpkin pies and roasted brussels sprouts, to do it up Viking style, slurp some ram testicles or chow down on *lundabaggar*, a sausage made from the butcher's leftovers (like colons), which are then rolled up, boiled, pickled, and sliced. No ranch dressing for dipping either, so nut up and swallow.

Continue feasting on the go by gnawing on a chunk of dried and fermented *hákarl* jerky; a shark that doesn't have a bladder so it pisses out of its skin. Another delicacy is *selshreifar*, or seal flippers, which are generally cured in lactic acid and taste like thick, chewy milk.

ISTANBUL

BREAKING THE FAST

During the Islamic holy month of Ramadan (Ramazan in Turkish), most religious followers fast from sun-up until sunset each day. A hypoglycemic's nightmare, fasting for Ramazan means that no food, drink, smoke, or even chewing gum can touch your lips during the daylight hours for thirty straight days. After going without food all day, the Turks are ready to chow by nightfall and Istanbul becomes one big raging dinner party, where people eat feverishly in preparation for the next day's empty stomach grumbles.

STARVING FOR A CAUSE

Each year Ramadan falls on the ninth month of the Islamic calendar. The Islamic calendar is based on moon cycles and only has 354 days, so the month of fasting moves back eleven days each year—beginning with the new moon. In the Quran, Allah states that all Muslims must fast during Ramadan as a way to make a personal sacrifice, reflect on living a life of virtue, and enter the New Year with greater spiritual purity. Fasting is considered one of the five pillars of Islam and all adult Muslims past puberty must practice the act of not eating. Hardcore followers also abstain from sex until they break the fast, compounding hunger and blue ball pangs into one, giant miserable feeling.

IFTAR: BREAK FAST OF CHAMPIONS

When the sun goes down, hungry Turks cure the pangs with a light meal known as *iftar*. Traditionally, the iftar meal begins with eating three dates followed by fresh pide bread, soup, pickled veggies, and olives. Nowadays, the iftar meal has turned into a hip affair throughout Istanbul, with one man trying to out-iftar the next in lavish displays of food and entertainment. Iftar tables are set up on many streets in every district of the city, hosting as many as 5,000 hungry people at a time and providing entertainment each night ranging from whirling dervish shows to poetry readings. In Sultanahmet Square, breaking the fast is celebrated each evening with traditional Turkish foods, tea, *nargile* (hookah) smoking, music, and candy-consuming. Wandering around the square is like putting yourself in a sensory wonderland—everything is delicious, filling and incredibly overwhelming.

LOUD, LATE NIGHT SNACKING

Your handful of midnight cookies pales in comparison to the kind of late-night snacking happening in these parts. *Sahur* is the big meal that is prepared and eaten in the middle of the night before sunrise. Around 2:30 a.m., drummers circle through the streets banging loud enough to get the whole city up and cookin'. The sahur meal usually begins with meat and a vegetable dish, followed by a pilaf or noodle dish and tied together with börek, thin, phyllo-like dough that's stuffed with a number of both sweet and savory fillings.

HERSHEY'S AND KISSES

When Ramadan ends, the good times of Ramadan Bayram (also known as the sugar/

candy feast) begin. In Turkey, Ramadan Bayram is like a three-day Halloween celebration, sans costumes, when kids go door-to-door screaming "Happy Bayram!" and are rewarded with candy, baklava (sweet, Turkish pastry), and sometimes money. The most important practice of Bayram, aside from OD-ing on sugar, is honoring the elderly. Being sweet to those older than yourself is observed by a ritual of kissing the right hand of elderly people and then placing the same hand on your forehead while uttering Bayram well wishes.

Should you choose to keep regular eating hours, don't be an insensitive prick and flaunt your food in front of fasters during Ramadan. Respect those that are saving themselves until the sun goes down and eat your meals inside a restaurant, café, or hoarder-style on the bottom bunk under the hostel blankets.

BAZAARO WORLD

Broke shopping in Istanbul is a lot more fun than it sounds, thanks to the Grand Bazaar and the Spice Bazaar. Even though it can be kind of touristy and over-priced, the Grand Bazaar is the largest and oldest covered market in the world with over 4,000 shops to browse where you can buy anything from an authentic carpet to a knockoff Gucci purse in any of the massive twenty-two buildings. As a bonus: feel free to pet any of the feral kitties outside the bazaar free of charge. The Spice Bazaar is the second-largest covered market in the world and the center of Istanbul's spice trade. Seeing the mounds of different colored spices in huge barrels doesn't cost anything and the weird mixture of smells is a free souvenir that you can keep in your nose for longer than you may wish.

FOOD FIGHT—NORTH VS. SOUTH

Way before hipsters and food evangelists cornered the term "locavore," Italians were munching on food picked from their yard, slaughtered in their kitchen, and caught at the bubbling streams they could see from their windows. The best food in the north or south is generally what grows well in the microclimate of that region. Italians like to keep their sons (cough)—mama's boys—(cough) and their food close to home. Northern Italy borders Switzerland, Austria, and France, so food there has more French and German influences than in the south, which is warmer and surrounded by the sea. As such, asking a northern Italian for lasagna (a southern dish) should elicit some unpleasant hand gestures. Read up on the great food divide so you can food slut your way around Italy without any nasty bumps.

DIRTY SOUTH

If your privates get public when you think about pizza and pasta, head down to the south, where their giant, juicy tomatoes make the Catholic schoolgirls blush. If you're gonna bust buttons on one city's streets, let it be Naples. More than anywhere else in Italy, Naples will pound you proper with its sweet dough and cheese. After tearing into a pizza at a standby, like L'Antica Pizzeria da Michele, make your sweet tooth ache at the many kiosks and tiny open-storefront bakeries. Get good and creamed with *zeppoli* (deep-fried dough balls, often filled with sweetened ricotta, pastry cream, or custard) and *sfogliatelle* (crunchy, pleated shell-shaped pastries usually filled with sweet ricotta).

NAUGHTY NORTH

If you dig cooler temps, cabbage and kale, and some blue-eyed blond(e)s with your Italian food, head up north, where the government isn't fucked up, and food is less likely to put you in a carb coma. In Venice, all that creeping around on canals has given the locals a taste for funked-out

PEACE WITH CHEESE

No discussion on Italian food would be complete without the lowdown on cheese. Ask the locals where to find the best cheese, and they'll respond, "*che il formaggio* (which cheese)?" If you're Italian, the world would end if your mozzarella came from the same city as your *parmigiano-reggiano*—the north and south produce two seriously different formaggio. The best *mozzarella di bufala* is from the southern Campania region, and the best parmigiano is—wait for it—in Parma (up north).

Italians get a little Godfather-y if you're ignorant about the food culture, so unless you want to find yourself dragged under a gondola or buried five-feet-deep in a Sicilian graveyard, we suggest you stop yapping and start swallowing that salami.

fish. *Baccalà mantecato* is salted, sometimes dried, creamed cod. Venetians pile into cramped *osterie* (quick, casual restaurants) or *bàcari* (wine bars, often with snacks), where there's just enough room for *cicheti* (appetizers). Served on toasty crostini, *baccalà* is a no-mayo-doused tuna fish sandwich. The cream is just the fish, pulverized and whipped into salty submission.

The Florentines, on the other hand, have been straight tripping since the fifteenth century, when peasants started getting down with all four cow stomachs. You'll know you're turning Italiano when you've acquired a taste for tripe—essentially, cattle stomach lining, which tastes just as rubbery as it sounds. If cow guts aren't your thing, chow down on *ribollita*, a black cabbage, root vegetable, and white bean soup that tastes like it's been blessed by the pope.

WORLD'S WACKIEST FOOD MUSEUMS

You already know that people chow down on some funky food around the world. But what does it take for a food to get its own museum? These weird-ass food shrines around the world prove that anything you can put on a plate can also be put on a pedestal.

Kimchi Field Museum
Seoul, South Korea

If you've ever smelled kimchi, the favorite fermented cabbage of the land, you'll understand how risky it is to make a tourist attraction out of it. This place displays the history of rubbing down cabbage with spices and fish paste and serves tiny samples at the end.

Kiwi360
Te Puke, New Zealand

We've met people from New Zealand who are offended when they're called fruit names such as "kiwi" (and sheep-fuckers for that matter), but it's undeniable that the country is filled with this fuzzy fruit. There's even a theme park dedicated to it where visitors are carted around kiwi fields and dropped off at a gift shop with kiwi-infused beauty products.

Coleman's Mustard Museum
Norwich, UK

While it's an iconic brand of mustard that first made an appearance in 1901, a whole museum dedicated to the condiment seems absurd. Somehow, though, this place has been profitably open since 1973. The gift shop has enough mustard to melt your face.

Vodka Museum
St. Petersburg, Russia

Vodka's not food, you say? Good luck telling that to a drunk Russian. Showcasing endless bottles of Russia's national treasure, this museum is attached to a restaurant where you can get your black and red caviar fix plus a few shots of the good stuff to chase down the fish eggs.

Momofuku Ando Instant Ramen Museum
Osaka, Japan

No, not delicious home-cooked ramen; this museum is dedicated to that shitty variety in a cup. Commissioned by Momofuku Ando, Instant Ramen's inventor, this place is all about that cup o' junk and you can make your own at the end choosing from 500 flavor options.

GEORGIA

HOW TO EAT YOUR WEIGHT IN BREAD

There's nothing Georgia-peachy about the street food in this former part of the Soviet Union. The Republic of Georgia has spent some seventy years cut off from the rest of the world, eating bread and cheese in every combination possible. Pick up all the delicious crumbs behind the Iron Curtain and bloat yourself into oblivion on the republic's kick-ass street cuisine.

KHACHAPURI

Bread and cheese: those two crazy kids go together like awesome and sauce. Georgians peddle this cheesy bread heaven—called *khachapuri*—across the country. The versions range from cheese-stuffed to cheese-topped and from flaky to über-bready. In the beach town of Batumi, things really get out of control with a boat-shaped variety filled with egg, butter, cheese, and more cheese. Forget Italians and Mexicans, Georgians are the iron chefs of artery-clogging.

TONIS PURI

Paleo freaks may as well jump off one of the country's massive mountain ranges if they plan to avoid bread in the ex-Commie country. Locals walking the streets stuffing their faces with fresh *tonis puri* (kiln bread) are about as common as hookers in Bangkok—and maybe equally as tempting. To get on the carb bandwagon, look for the typical hole-in-the-wall bakeries marked with the word "t'one." Pronounced "toe-nay," this means the bakery is equipped with an old-school clay oven that pops out hot bread all day.

KHINKALI

Save up some cash and splurge on a sit-down meal to try one of the country's most famous dishes: *khinkali*. Essentially fatty dim sum, the doughy-pouched dumplings are a spiced-meat-and-oozy-juice party in your mouth. Unlike their Chinese counterpart, these more gigantic versions are served in mass quantities to satisfy even the most raging case of the munchies.

OTP Tip: To eat it like the locals, first slurp up the liquid insides by holding the *khinkali* by the top and taking a bite from the bottom.

LOBIANI

Just when you thought you could totally live without refried beans, Georgia reignites your gassy passion for the cafeteria slop. The country's answer to the bean burrito—*lobiani*—comes stuffed, yet again, in more bread. All that's missing is some tequila and a side of guac.

KADA

Basically just piecrust coiled up for easy inhaling purposes, this buttery pastry is usually served at stands and bakeries. Expect it to go straight to your ass.

CUT THROUGH THE CARBS WITH KEBAB

Georgia's version of cheap street food looks like your typical lump of mystery meat but gets its local flare from a mixture of cilantro and unique spices. Down your kebab with a side of tomato sauce called *satsebeli*. With other meaty dishes, though, opt for *tkemali*, an herbalicious plum sauce that Georgians equate to ketchup. Eating a kebab is a great way to add a little protein to that monster loaf baking in your stomach.

No matter how nice the porcelain is, always expect a hangover after a night of drinking bathtub wine. *Borjomi*, Georgia's miracle mineral water produced in the town of the same name, collects five miles underground as a byproduct of earth's magma, and volcanic gas bubbles it slowly upward, picking up minerals along the way and mixing it with ground water. A mile beneath the surface, the long journey ends as it feeds into the town of Borjomi's spring wells. Borjomi is said to boost the immune system, ease digestive issues, increase metabolism, prevent cavities, replenish electrolytes, treat diabetes, and, of course, cure hangovers. So, when you're suffering from the wrath of this country's unfiltered grapes, know that Mother Earth has been cooking up your cure for 1,500 years.

WINE

If bread is the go-to grub, then wine is the go-to booze—Georgians actually claim they invented it and famously toast endlessly with the homemade, unfiltered concoction, which is a murky yellow in color. While more refined wines exist, the homebrew version is popular at most restaurants.

STROKE THIS!

Churchkhela

So eating something that resembles a dildo covered in anal beads won't be weird at all, right? The Georgians don't think so. This funky little joystick has been coined the "Georgian Snickers"—what with its hand-held convenience and nutty interior. Don't expect it to be all sweet and chocolaty though. Instead, the Eurasian street-treat—often found in other countries throughout the region—tastes more like nuts covered in a fruit roll-up.

BANH YOURSELF PHO REALS!

A few years back, Vietnamese cuisine was something only its people and a small handful of food-savvy non-Asians knew much about. Today, it has become one of the trendiest stateside ethnic foods. While any Yelp-user can whip up a list of "authentic" Vietnamese restaurants in Seattle, Santa Ana, or Houston, why not one-up them by hightailing it to the motherland instead?

BANH

Any food item containing the word "banh" means it's flour-based, and there's no better way to kick-start the day than with a huge plate of carbs. Out of all the yeasty treats, the most popular is the *banh mi*, a crispy baguette stuffed with your choice of cold cuts, grilled or roasted pork, pâté, pickled carrots and daikon, cilantro, chili peppers, cucumbers, buttered mayo, eggs, or all of the above.

Another popular *banh* variety is the *banh xeo*, a giant savory Vietnamese crêpe packed with fatty pork, shrimp, mint leaves, basil, and bean sprouts, pan-fried over a charcoal burner and topped off with *nuoc mam* (that delicious, foul-smelling fish sauce). Available at all banh xeo-only restaurants on Tuyen Quang Street (a.k.a. Banh Xeo Street) in Phan Thiet, listen for the loudest sizzles to pick your dispensary.

PHO SHO!

Forget that shitty ramen you lived on as a starving college kid. When it comes to noodles, the Vietnamese don't mess with that Cup-o'-junk. Instead, warm up your spoon for some *pho* (pronounced "fuh" not "foh"), a steaming-hot bowl of vermicelli noodle soup served with beef or chicken, bean sprouts, basil, and cilantro. Spice it up with some chili peppers, a squirt of lime juice, and Sriracha.

If your broth ends up a bright red from all that Sriracha, congrats! You've graduated to *bun bo Hue*, a spicier, sassier pho variety from central Vietnam. This lemongrass-laden noodle soup comes loaded with marinated beef, sliced cabbage, raw onions, oxtail, pork knuckles, and congealed pig's blood—if you're no Bourdain, you can ask them to hold the last two.

ROLL UP

For a light midday snack, grab some *goi cuon*, or spring rolls. The main ingredients—pork, shrimp, lettuce, vermicelli noodles, and fresh herbs—are wrapped in delicate rice paper and served in a neat, easy-to-manhandle bundle. Dip it in some peanut hoisin sauce and try to avoid looking vulgar as you shove it in your mouth whole.

SWEETS

Feed your food baby one last time with some *che*, a dessert beverage or pudding usually made with some variation of fruit, beans, and sticky rice. One of the most

SNAKE VILLAGE

For a special evening out, grab a glass of *ruou ran*, or snake wine. Take your pick of steeped wine, where snakes are soaked in the wine for several months before it is served, or mixed wine, in which the snake gets sliced down the belly and its blood is drained into a delicious shot glass of wine. Don't worry—ethanol in the wine denatures the snake venom, so you won't have to call a medic. Hit up one of the many slithery snake wine bars in Le Mat (or Snake Village) outside of Hanoi. Fang-fucking-tastic!

TEST YOUR GAG REFLEXES

Most Americans probably frown upon consuming a pseudofetus, but it's totally the norm in Southeast Asia. Locals eat the shit out of fertilized duck and chicken eggs, known as *trung vit lon* in Vietnam. How it's done:

Take a partially incubated egg, boil it for twenty minutes, crack it open with a spoon, and enjoy the savory flavor of an aborted bird fetus. These wildly popular embryonic treats are typically sold by rowdy street vendors and are a late-night favorite among drunken revelers. Forget all the other weird stuff they hawk on the streets down there; trung vit lon is the ultimate food challenge and comes with foodie bragging rights (as long as you omit the part about puking feathers all afternoon).

commonly consumed is *che sam bo luong*, a sweet, cold soup made with lotus seeds, sliced seaweed, red jujubes, dried longans, Job's tears (a grain native to Southeast Asia), and crushed ice.

FINISH OFF WITH A COLD ONE

Vietnamese people aren't big drinkers in general (damn that Asian red-face-inducing, lack-of-alcohol-digestion-gene!), but they still know how to enjoy a drink or two. Each region has a local draft beer named after it (Bia Saigon, Bia Can Tho, etc.), and deciding which one's best comes down to the drinker's own taste. If price outweighs taste, the cheapest beer in the land is Bia Hoi, at under twenty-five cents a pint.

MUSIC

Every country has distinct musical roots, and globalization has remixed the world's music scene into some interesting sounds. From regional musical superstars, globally intertwined genres, live festivals, and the busking culture, the music of the world is best experienced live. Pick up a fiddle and jam in Belfast with the drunkest musicians on the planet, or shed a tear to the sad *fado* tunes in Portugal. While we can tell you everything we know about hip-hop in Senegal, it's up to you to get out there and actually feel the bass thumping yourself.

BELFAST

SINGING WITH THE IRISH— WHEN BOOZE AND TUNES COLLIDE

Many of Belfast's pubs have been hosting the drunk and rowdy since the seventeenth century. In these historic pubs, you can warm up and listen to traditional Irish music for free, until you're ready to join in and lend your vocal cords to a little Irish bending. You will emerge feeling like the winner of *American Idol* and smelling like an alleyway on St. Patrick's Day.

LOOKING FOR TREBLE TROUBLE

You can find Irish music almost any night of the week. Some sessions begin with a few musicians, and as the night (and the pints) go on, others will often join in. These are called "traditional sessions," and, as you may expect, most musicians take a long Guinness break between every song. Occasionally, you might see a fight or a jig break out; in either case you can join in or sit back and watch.

IRISH INSTRUMENTS

Your Jameson-flooded eyes aren't playing tricks on you; the Irish are known to have some funky music makers. Uilleann pipes are kind of like bagpipes except the air is pumped with the elbow instead of the mouth—sure, it looks goofy, but the Irish bust out some quality jams on these

things. You also might see a pear-shaped, guitar-like instrument known as a *bouzouki*. This thing came to Ireland in the mid-'60s from Greece and is now a staple in Irish jigs. To round out the band, flutes, fiddles, harps, and accordions will all chime in.

JIGGA WHERE?

Madden's has the best Guinness, features sessions almost every night, and brings in a mostly local crowd. You have to buzz the door for entry, a relic of the days when the Protestant/Unionists would attack Catholic/Nationalist pubs and vice versa. Around the corner is seedier Kelly's Cellar pub, where you won't have trouble finding a fight to go with your pint. Aside from being the oldest building in the city of Belfast, McHugh's is one of the big daddies in food and music, and has an early-bird session on Saturday afternoons. The Garrick is aces for pub grub and for catching a few football (soccer) matches before the music begins.

Drunken Irishmen and musical instruments are the hallmark of any successful trip to the Emerald Isle. If you haven't hugged a few leprechaun-lovers, sung yourself into hoarse oblivion, and drunk enough Guinness to turn your stomach into an Easy-Bake Oven by the end of your trip, stock up on lucky charms and try again.

THE WORLD'S MOST POPPIN' MUSIC VENUES

No need to hold your iPod earbuds deep into your ears any longer. Pack a lighter and hop on the OTP tour bus; these venues will crank up the volume to a level you've never heard before.

Slane Castle, Ireland
Situated along the River Boyne, this castle's grounds sport enough room for 80,000 loyal tune junkies to get their high-quality fix.

Sydney Opera House, Australia
Like the Eiffel Tower in France, this award-winning arts building has become the face of Australia. Don't let the name fool you; there's plenty of awesome music to munch on other than opera.

Red Rocks Amphitheater, Colorado
Sandwiched between two 300-foot sandstone rocks, Red Rocks' stage was built by Mother Nature and approved by countless music-loving humans.

Harpa Concert Hall, Iceland
A geometric wonder inspired by the island nation's picturesque landscape, this venue is decked out in colored glass that brings the wondrous outside in. Titillate your ears here during the Iceland Airwaves Festival, when Harpa clinks glasses for five full days in early November.

Dalhalla, Sweden
A rockin' venue made entirely of rocks, Dalhalla soundtracks summertime in Sweden. The thin moat that separates the stage from the crowd means you better bring a board if you intend to crowd surf.

CUBA

RUMP SHAKIN'

Mamis and papis from Havana to Guantanamo prowl and wink and love and dance from dawn till dusk. A necessity for pleasure, work, and everything in between, music is to daily life what foreplay is to sex—and room-by-the-hour hotels are more common than Coca-Cola in Cuba.

THE BEAT BEGINS

Cuban girls learn to gyrate before they have hips, and mambos, pachangas, and bachatas flow through the blood of every Cuban human. The 1940s were the Golden Age of Cuban music, when gangsters in furs driving "Yank Tanks" rolled up to the Buena Vista Social Club to swap cigars and get laid. The nightclub is still hedonism's headquarters, even if dancing styles have changed. You can forget the salsa lessons if you're hitting the scene—today's merengue and reggaeton bumps and grinds more like hip-hop.

SHAKE IT UP!

Cuban nightclubs may be responsible for some unplanned pregnancies, and no one

THE COOLEST OLD DUDES AROUND

In 1997, Cuba's bloodless music revolution hit the world stage with the sexiest, sultriest Latin album ever released, making "salsa" and "Cuba Libres" household words. *Buena Vista Social Club* was an all-star album, featuring Cuban voices and songs that helped conceive a generation. For some of the musicians on the album, its release was their first public performance since being silenced by Castro.

The compilation album is named after the infamous club in Havana, where many of its performers were top-bill names. After the album dropped, the rechristened "Buena Vista Social Club" performers were invited to play on exclusive stages from Amsterdam to New York. Eight of the original twenty-two members have gone up to that big band in the sky, but the group still tours. Most members are older than your granddaddy, but they pound on bongos, blow into trumpets, strum guitars, and feverishly deliver lyrics with intense, passionate energy.

COINLESS CASINO

It takes mad moves to get lucky at a Cuban Casino. Back in the day, people went to *casinos*, or Cuban dance halls, to roll their hips, not the dice. When the casinos were closed during the revolution, the style of salsa developed there took the name. Cuban salsa—casino—is a flirtatious game inspired by the *sabor*, the feeling and flavor, of the music.

The first casino was danced in the 1950s, and combined the rhythm of mambo with Afro-Cuban rumba moves. It's said that in salsa, the man is "the frame to the woman's picture," but casino is a deck both sexes deal. It's an interaction between dance partners and, like in rumba, highlights the small sensuality of a wrist-flick or hip-twist. *Despelote* is a tease performed between partners who shimmy and shake close enough to shag, but whose bodies never touch.

Other types of salsa are danced linearly and—for music theory geeks—on the upward beat. When Cuba was isolated during the Cuban embargo, casino was allowed to develop without other Latin influence. It's danced on a downward beat (1-3-5) and partners face each other in a circular motion. The *rueda* (wheel) *de casino* is unique to Cuban salsa. An emcee calls out sultry moves and partners are swapped like a big Latin hoedown. Traditional rueda de casino is less formal than the bastardized Miami version.

Suelta, a type of casino performed individually that features fast footwork and elaborate gesticulations, is best seen on a stage in Havana or Santiago de Cuba. If the masters have you itching for a go, take a twirl on the floor at hotspots like Club 1830 in Havana.

can say they don't bring the ass-thumping dance full force. Havana and Santiago de Cuba are the island's dance hubs. Get down and dirty at Havana's El Chévere, an open-air reggaeton club with an open bar special. If you're trying to get fancy in the capital city, slip on those heels and hit up a live reggaeton show at Café Cantante Mi Habana.

FLOCKS OF FUN

If you're looking for some girl-girl, boy-boy, or boy-girl-girl-boy action, Havana is where it's at. The *pajaritos* of Cuba, a saucy, endearing term for gays that means "little bird," know how to party. *"Fiestas de diez pesos"* are roaming LGBT dance parties that typically cost 10 pesos. Hang out along the Malecón and keep an ear to the street to find out where it'll go down.

DOWNTEMPO

Despite the island's thumping bass line, Cubans can chill with the best of them and music is an important component to relaxation. Traditional café Cubanos serve up sexy *charangas*—traditional music ensembles—as a matter of course. Smaller towns, such as Trinidad or Vinales, are better for intimate performances. Café Cantante in Santiago bills killer salsa and bolero music, and the city's Casa del Caribe keeps it classy with Afro-Cuban, Latin, and Caribbean performances. Shit goes nearly 24/7 at the Casa de la Musica in Havana, so you can move hard, then pass out to hot jams all in the same place and without skipping a beat.

No matter how you get down, moving your body is a Cuban test of virility, and the beat of the country pulses from the Gulf of Mexico to the Caribbean Sea.

IGLOOFEST

A city known better for its hockey than its party scene, Montreal opens its doors to thousands of drunken rave seekers during Igloofest and encourages everyone to party themselves stupid in the dead of winter. Held on the water, Igloofest is a rave in the name of all things freezing and fun. Join 10,000 French Canadians wearing their most ridiculous ski suits on the streets of Old Montreal and follow them down to the water to dance off the hypothermia.

FREEZE FRAME

From a distance all you can see are glowing lights and massive blocks of ice. Coming closer, the bass hits your eardrums as the party body count begins to rise. If you're down to dance and have a good time, Montreal is happy to play host to whatever level of debauchery you bring them (as long as you don't bitch about the cold).

Ice sculptures and monstrous, brightly colored, glowing fake igloos cover the festival grounds. There are tug-of-war and best ski suit contests, open fires for roasting marshmallows, and more Jaeger and

Sapporo than anyone could ever drink, even with 10,000 friends.

Every Thursday, Friday, and Saturday throughout January, Igloofest rages on with new DJs from all around the globe. They're so dedicated to the winter theme that even the DJs' table is made entirely of ice blocks. The lights and lasers reflect off the falling snow and ice to create a stunning visual experience. At Igloofest, the music comes second to the good times and since the music is usually on-point, good times turn into great times quick.

PROUD TO BE CANADIAN

Canadians love their country and show off what they have to offer front and center. The party isn't happening at some open field outside the city limits, but practically downtown, right on the river in Old Montreal. To preserve some Canadian pride, for every globe-trotting DJ that spins at Igloofest, there is a local Canadian DJ spinning the same night on the same stage. Playing host to a rave for 10,000-plus EDM party animals automatically makes you cooler than, say, Lincoln, Nebraska. In addition to throwing a great party, Montreal's winter bars kick ass. Check out the Dominion Tavern on Metcalfe Street. With large leather booths lining the walls, this bar is like taking the DeLorean back about 100 years. The whole thing is made of ancient oak and manned by skilled bartenders who only need sleeve belts to complete their Golden Age getup. They've got enough scotch in there to give you hallucinations of a scribbling Mark Twain posted up in the corner.

HAULIN' ASS AROUND TOWN

Buried deep below the ground, the subway often looks more like something from *Lord of the Rings* than an entrance to mass transit. But five escalators later, you arrive at a clean, concise, and fast metro system that will get you anywhere you might need to go within the city limits. While there is no shortage of cabs or buses, the subway system is legit and will haul your confused ass anywhere you need to be. As far as staying in the city for the festival, since Igloofest is downtown, there are many hostel options only a few subway stops away from the action.

Perhaps Igloofest is an überpolite way for Montreal to say, "fuck you, ay!" to America. We poke fun at their pronunciation of "about," but when it comes to cold weather partying, Montreal has America beat big time. While we sit inside counting dust bunnies and waiting for spring, in Montreal, they embrace the winter freeze, marching down to the coldest part of their city to drink, dance, and share good times with thousands of brave strangers.

WHAT THE F*CK IS FADO?

Fado, literally translated, means "prophecy," "fate," or "destiny." Culturally, it is known as the "soul of Portugal." A heart-wrenching form of musical poetry, fado is a style of song that came out of tiny Portugal's big-shot days, when explorers set off to sea to discover new lands while the women they left behind longingly wailed across the water, awaiting their return. If you're ever feeling homesick abroad, gather yourself and find some solidarity with fado.

SOUNDS LIKE . . .

Influenced by former Portuguese colonies—as well as North African jams—and blended with Portuguese poetry and urban folk tradition, the music is haunting and evocative (something like a blend of mellow Hawaiian tunes and flamenco), and embraces the concept of *saudade*, roughly interpreted as "melancholy." A twelve-string Portuguese guitar that looks like a knocked-up banjo traditionally backs the vocals.

HEY, WHO FADO-ED?

Portugal wasn't always so embracing of fado—at one point it was predominantly sung by prostitutes in brothels and considered evil. These days you'll find legit *fadistas* singing in the Moorish Alfalma district in Lisbon. Fado performances are generally held in dimly lit taverns known as *casas de fado*, which are bare bones in terms of acoustics. It's considered impolite and distracting to the fadista to eat while she or he is singing, and the food at these joints tends to be on the crappy side anyway.

POKE AROUND PORTUGAL

Take a road trip down to the University town of Coimbra, where the fado has a different flavor. Coimbra fado is more likely to be sung by a man or men (vs. women in Lisbon), and because the town is all about university

smarts, the musical style is more affiliated with the intellectual class than its blue-collar counterpart in the capital. Check out the Fado ao Centro (Fado Center) for an inexpensive and enlightening performance. Round out your folk-music vacation in Oporto, where you can sip some thick and sweet fortified port wine. Let out the last of your sobs at Casa da Mariquinhas, the oldest and best-known fado house in Oporto.

KNOW YOUR FADO

If you get into a fado name-dropping predicament, Amália Rodrigues, who sang in the Lisbon style, is an important one to know. Early in Rodrigues's career, she began renovating fado's melodies, modernizing them, and setting some to sixteenth-century poems by Luís de Camões. While many fado traditionalists criticized this finagling with the classics, most came to love her, and she is now considered the "Queen of Fado," as well as a national icon.

THE BIGGEST, LOUDEST, AND WILDEST MUSIC FESTIVALS AROUND THE WORLD

Summer months set the mood for amped-up, outdoor music festivals. Peep some of these world-class events and party like a rock star.

Roskilde: Denmark
Over 100,000 heads rock to big-name punk, rock, and metal bands from Scandinavia and beyond in this four-day event in Denmark.

All Tomorrow's Parties: England
No corporate sponsors? No problem. This British alternative to the almighty Glastonbury Festival doesn't draw as big of a crowd, but we like the friendly vibes that arise from performers and fans partying together.

Exit: Serbia
Southeast Europe's largest cultural crowd gathers in Novi Sad (Serbia's second-largest city), flooding its seventeenth-century Petrovaradin fortress with over 250,000 festival-goers annually.

Coachella: USA
Spread over two 3-day weekends, California's Coachella showcases everything from mainstream hip-hop to grunge. Expect girls in booty shorts, celebrities, and a gnarly sunburn if you're not careful.

Gnaoua: Morocco
Located in the city of Essaouira, this is a freebie festival where you get tons more than you pay for. The beats that flow through the sea of sound are called "gnawa" and put the half-million-strong crowd into a happy, ready-to-dance trance.

SENEGAL

HIP-HOP PIONEERS

The youth of Senegal have been busting beats since the '80s. Today, they're influencing the rest of the African continent to hop to their hips. A genre that has traditionally been defined by money, cars, and clothes, hip-hop here is a cultural movement covering the social and political life in Senegal (kind of the way New York originally intended it to be). Let the sound in, see your thoughts spin, and get to know the Senegalese flow.

HOW IT ALL STARTED

Before lyrical assassins started murdering drum-filled, bouncy beats, the musically-inclined nation of Senegal had *griots*. These were a respected people—separated into their own caste—who were responsible for speaking about society through song. Oral historians and cultural traditionalists, griots would sing anywhere and about everything; like Twitter, if it was trending, they were covering it. With Senegal becoming more modernized by the mid 1980s, its youth yearned for a new voice. Griots faded out and hip-hop artists came in.

THE RAP

Think of Senegal's capital city of Dakar as the impact point of a hip-hop bomb that exploded with flavor and rapidly produced new artists. Senegal's artists use the past to light their bright future as they are influenced largely by hip-hop's beginnings in the South Bronx. The native Wolof tongue (along with French and English) is used to produce raps that cover all kinds of serious shit like crime, corruption, HIV/AIDS, poverty, and ethnic strife. Beats are often backed by the banging of traditional Senegalese drums and—more so than American hip-hop—the art form is widely heard, appreciated, and understood.

WHO YOU SHOULD KNOW

Daara J (meaning "the school of life") is a group of artists who draw on cultural diversity to get their messages to appeal to the masses. Papa Moussa Lo, better known as "Waterflow," uses his hip-hop talents to be the voice of the voiceless. The duo who comprise PBS (Positive Black Soul) take a similar approach by rapping their positive, feel-good stories in French, English, and Wolof. Africulturban—a cultural center for hip-hop founded by famed Senegalese rapper Matador—holds free hip-hop festivals to get young people into the groove. People across the continent love to bob their heads to the beats and listen to the thought-provoking lyrics. Hip-hop can change the here and now, and Senegal is a perfect example of where and how.

=== *Fun Fact* ===

Ever heard of Touré Kunda? No? What about Carlos Santana? Santana's "Africa Bamba," a hit on his überpopular *Supernatural* album, was actually a reworking of "Guerilla Africa," a song by Senegalese group Touré Kunda.

KARAOKE HEADQUARTERS

With an estimated two million Koreans channeling their inner Beyoncé each day, there is no better way to sing to the song of a local in Seoul than getting wasted and belting out some utterly embarrassing tune in the company of friends and strangers.

STARTING OFF WITH A NORAEBANG

Invented in Japan in the 1970s, karaoke traveled to Korea in the 1980s and never left. Koreans refer to karaoke as *noraebang* or "song room," which is exactly where you'll be going with your falsetto-fabulous Korean friends in Seoul. A private room designed for you to pretend like you're on an arena stage in front of five to thirty of your new besties, noraebangs are everywhere in Seoul and easy to spot even if you don't read Korean: just look for a neon sign with a microphone or musical symbol.

NAME THAT TUNE

After a long binge out on the town, head to a noraebang, where you can sing your heart out until someone's ears bleed. The monster songbooks are normally filled with thousands of songs in Korean and English (a few German songs might be thrown in there, too). This is the time to drop your inhibitions and embrace your pop princess. Don't fret if you need backup; most rooms are equipped with two microphones. If you really get into the groove, pick up one of the tambourines that come with most rooms and add a little jangle to your jingle. Copious amounts of *soju* (and snacks) are brought to the room and they keep liquid courage on tap so you can squeal and shimmy until sunrise.

WE ALL SCREAM FOR NORAEBANG

Each noraebang in Seoul is an opportunity to enter a unique, themed wonder-world of amateur song. If you really want to go out with a bang, hit up Luxury, a noraebang in Hongdae, which looks like a ginormous, neon dollhouse. If singing in Barbie's dream house isn't enough, Luxury offers free ice cream! Feeling furry? The noraebang History001 near Konkuk University gives you an opportunity to wear animal costumes while singing. They also offer free ice cream! You scream, I scream—just try not to scream in the microphone.

JUST SOJU KNOW

Russians have vodka, Americans have Budweiser, and Koreans have soju. The most popular spirit in Korea has been getting peeps in the party mood since the thirteenth century.

Traditionally distilled from rice, nowadays soju is often combined with another grain—like wheat or barley—and even comes in fruity flavors like apple. It's most commonly enjoyed in large groups with food. Remember to mind your soju manners, kids: two hands are better than one when offering, accepting, and drinking; and *your* hands should never pour your own glass—out of respect, let someone else do the dirty work.

SEX AND PARTYING

All differences aside, everyone in the world likes a good party (and good sex). Party under the glow of the full moon in Thailand, thumb through a huge collection of sex toys in Paris' Pigalle, and rage on to Carnaval in Brazil, the big, feathery granddaddy of street parties. Often, you don't even have to leave your hostel to party, as many places cater to the backpacker party beast that gets unleashed the minute you step on foreign territory. With so many party possibilities, the world's party scene will make stateside weekend ragers feel like weak sauce. International hookups are bound to happen, and global great times are guaranteed.

BERLIN

COMMUNAL DRUNKFESTS

Like twins conjoined at the skull, separating Germany and beer would result in a bloody mess. Not a place to fuck around when it comes to brew, Berlin is a history-soaked place in northern Germany where beer drinking is also a varsity sport and biergartens, beer bars, and festivals provide countless options for saturation.

FROTHY CULTURE

While their famous blond lagers have only been around for 150 years, Germans have been brewing beer for at least 3,000 years. They're so psychotic about their beer that special laws were created surrounding its production. The *Reinheitsgebot*, or the German Beer Purity Law, states that beer only equals water, barley, and hops. This ensures that every brewer gets a level playing field and eliminates the possibility of drinking a six-pack of elephant piss (we're looking at you, Bud Light). Despite the rigidity of what goes into their beer, the consumption laws are surprisingly lax. In Berlin, there are no open-container laws, so the U-Bahn, S-Bahn, streets, squares, parks, and everywhere in between become a virtual beer garden. That's great news for cheap travelers who want to hang out with a tallboy and skip the bars altogether.

BEER THE BERLIN WAY

Take the class up just a half notch to fully marinade in Berlin's beer culture. Strict beerophiles go to Berlin in August. Like Oktoberfest, the "Internationales Berliner Bierfestival" brings together drunks from all over the world annually. It also butts up to the Munich event, so the opportunity to get shitfaced for an entire month and annoy a large portion of the German population is within reach. Beer chugging is basically a national sport, and putting on your beer goggles first thing in the morning is perfectly acceptable.

For the slightly more ambitious, try the Fat Tire Bike Tour, a great way to burn beer calories while pedaling your way toward more beer. You'll get to stop at a biergarten for lunch, and if you're in no mood for *spaetzle* or *weisswurst* solids, you're totally allowed to maintain a liquid diet. Loretta's Biergarten and Café am Neuen See in the Tiergarten have large trees and tons of tables with intermixed beer and food stalls, and are perfect for outdoor re-dehydration. Here, you can get nice and hammered, then rent a rowboat on the adjacent lake.

There's no scarcity of beer-infused shenanigans in Berlin. So go on—make the Spree River appear a pale shade of gold, and rock out with your stein out.

WHEN ALL YOU WANT TO DO IS DANCE!

Berlin is known for its massive club scene. The more popular places (like Tresor and Berghain) are usually expensive and picky about whom they let past the door. Make the yeast in your stomach dance till the sun rises at OTP's backpacker club picks:

White Trash
The typical posh club's grimy cousin, this place has decent burgers, a club on-site, and, usually, live music in the bar area. Their beer is cheap, and it's right in the middle of the city.

Cassiopeia
Named after a constellation, Cassiopeia has an outside garden, and the music is normally electronica or drum/bass. This place also packs a rock-climbing wall for when you decide to let drunken Indiana Jones take the reins.

Club der Visionäre
Rumored to have some of the best pizza in Berlin, this Kreuzberg club on a river barge has a mild identity crisis. Sort of a fancy club with a tinge of grungy riverside bar/restaurant, it's perfect for grabbing a slice and swaying side to side until the drowsies set in.

EVERYTHING YOU NEED TO KNOW ABOUT CARNAVAL

Arguably the greatest party on the planet, Rio's Carnaval falls right at the top of every partier's puke-bucket list. Every February or March, from the Friday about fifty days before Easter until the Tuesday before Lent, thousands of bodies flock to join *cariocas* (Rio locals) for this five-day exhibition of excess. It's easy to get lost in the chaos of colors, parades, and street parties. Let's sift through this blur of samba, skin, insomnia, and sex.

PREPARE

Coming from the United States, you'll dish out at least a grand for your high-season flight down to the "Marvelous City." Hotels and hostels in Copacabana and Ipanema shake you down for at least quadruple their normal rates and often demand full-week stays. You might do better on apartment-rental sites like Airbnb.com, but

unless you're lucky enough to score a couch to surf, expect to pay a pretty penny for the very little sleep you'll get. To avoid sleeping on the sidewalk of N.S. Copacabana Avenue, booking early is mandatory. You'll even notice the restaurant prices are all written in chalk so owners can jack them up during the festival. There's no way around it—Carnaval is expensive. You may have to finally take a hammer to your piggy bank, but trust us; it's worth every one of those pennies. Now, let's get you a party plan.

SAMBA PARADES

Massive, mind-boggling floats, "who the fuck comes up with this shit?" costumes, gyrating g-strings, and all the samba music your eardrums can handle await you in the Sambadrome—the half-mile-long permanent parade grounds. If you've seen pictures of Carnaval, chances are they were taken in one of the neighborhood camps known as "samba schools," where cariocas somehow manage to stay relatively naked while wearing extravagant costumes. From Saturday to Tuesday, a year of preparation culminates in a ninety-minute march, during which samba schools fiercely compete for the awe of fans and the votes of judges.

BRAZILIANS HAVE BUTTS IN THE BAG

While there is a lot of nice ass out in the world, Brazilians always get the Booty Olympic Gold. Whether it's all that late-night samba, or just raw natural talent, these butts wipe out the competition.

STREET PARTIES

Skip the pricey, Viagra-popper-infested black tie balls; the street parties are way more your style. In the center of these *bandas* and *blocos*, a percussion circle pumps out nonstop samba music. Brazilians shuffle their feet and shake their asses as vendors wheel around rickety coolers of cheap beer and caipirinhas. There is no dress code, so dress up, dress down, or barely dress at all. Pick up a few samba steps and join the masses (but watch your wallet!). Check out "Simpatia é quase amor," a street festival in Ipanema, and then head out to the Lapa neighborhood for a massive street party.

HOOK UP!

Start your tongue aerobics now, because these street parties are a saliva Swap-O-Rama. Young cariocas routinely make out with dozens of drooling hopefuls in a single night. All it takes is eye contact, an approach, and a few words before you are familiarizing yourself with some hot Brazilian's taste buds.

JUST CAN'T SWING IT?

If Rio's Carnaval just isn't in the budget, fret not. Carnaval is not just a Rio holiday; it's a national holiday, celebrated throughout Brazil. Street parties pop up in towns across the country with less tourism (which means lowered costs).

If timing is the issue, you can still get a Carnaval cock-tease at a samba school rehearsal. Starting in August, the schools rehearse on weekend nights, with the band practicing its samba beats and the crowds warming up their shuffling feet. The entrance and drinks are cheap, and the cariocas are all too willing to welcome their new gringo friends with *beijos*.

COPENHAGEN

KINKY COPENHAGEN

Scandinavia is scandalous as fuck! Copenhagen is known for its legal prostitution—which was decriminalized in 1999—and loose attitudes about sex. A place where you can jerk off at strip clubs, Copenhagen didn't get to be the most attractive city for nudists by sitting around on its ass wearing pants. Bring your sex positivity and let your kink flag fly.

KINKSTORY

Copenhagen is seriously sexy, and in some ways you'd never imagine. Ever heard of dogging? It's the act of engaging in and/or watching sexual activity in public—there are unofficial spots in the city's public parks where people go at it, legally.

Copenhagen is great if you're gay; trans; into BDSM; like sexy dungeons, rent-by-the-hour love hotels, swinger bars, brothels, or sex clubs—whatever your thing(s), Copenhagen's got the goods and an entire festival dedicated to kink.

DEETS ON TEETS

Kinky Copenhagen is a festival held every October to showcase the best in sex fetishes from BDSM and more obscure obsessions. Got a redhead fetish? Welcome to paradise. Like to eat grilled cheese sandwiches from the strange crevices of other people's bodies? Can probably make it happen here. You bet your balls there will be strippers, dominatrices, porn stars, and dudes with whips dressed in latex. Even if you like your sex vanilla, this is the place to breathe easy and let go.

TATS ON TEETS

The kinkfest comes with other perks. Tattoo artists set up shop amid the sexiness, and if your inhibitions are on the next flight out to never-never land, you can get tattoos done right at the fest. If you're more into piercing and shoving hooks into your skin in general, the fest is a body modification wonderland where you can get anything from a simple nose ring to dragon spikes inserted down your spine. Embracing impulse not your forte? Copenhagen has world-renowned tattoo parlors like the Meat Shop and Royal Tattoo—where legend Henning Jørgensen has been doing his handiwork for over thirty years.

HIPPIE HIDEAWAY

If you get sick of sexfestin', Christiania is a unique commune inside Copenhagen that was started by hippies fifty years ago. The place is covered in murals, smells like a cloud of weed, and is a happy getaway from the city bustle. The main drag here is Pusher Street, and while hard drugs are prohibited, you can get a handful of greens for cheap and chill knowing that guns and cars are prohibited in this community-owned property.

OTP Tip: Want kink right fucking now? You only have to travel as far as wild and wacky San Francisco where every September, the streets are alive with the sound of bullwhips at the Folsom Street Fair.

TOPLESS BEACH MECCA

With all of Greece's beauty, lack of inhibition, and cultural love of food, it's no wonder that the country is one of the horniest in the world. Best observed topless and beachside, Greeks are a unique, fun-loving bunch. Sneak a peek at OTP's three favorite Greek topless beaches.

RED BEACH, CRETE

Crete's best beach requires a bit of a hike to access (the reward is lots of nudity, so suck it up and trek on). Signs will point you toward the beach from anywhere in Matala, eventually leading you to a goat's path that you'll hike downhill for a solid fifteen minutes. Once you've made it to the beach, leave your clothes and inhibitions behind, and embrace one of Greece's greatest topless (and then some) beaches. Awesomely convenient caves line the ocean and provide perfect seclusion for your own body-inspection station.

PARADISE BEACH, MYKONOS

Join the masses from all over the world as they unite to celebrate life. You've heard of "letting loose"—take a trip to Paradise Beach and you might turn to liquid. This place is the wonderful result of combining Greece's natural beauty with nonstop partying. Forget about partying like a rock star—come here to rage like a boulder supernova.

MYRTOS BEACH, KEFALONIA

In the northwest corner of Kefalonia lies Myrtos Beach, often regarded as the best beach in Greece. At first glance, it may seem like nothing special, but its sea of shimmery water, surrounded by green mountains, all swallowed by a beating sun

are the winning ingredients for the perfect beach. Feel free to even out your tan lines and let your eyes wander.

OTP Tip: Fancy hotel bars dominate the night-life scene in Greece and make for perfect hook-up spots. In Athens, check out Galaxy at the Hilton, where the sunset view is arguably all the sex you'll need; the backpacker-macker hot spot Hoxton, where you can hook up with your own backpacker breed; or Mike's, if karaoke is your idea of foreplay.

LEGENDARY PUBS

It's no secret that Londoners know how to get down with the drink, and have been not-so-quietly chugging pints for centuries. While a watering hole is never more than a stone's throw away, these London pubs are legendary libation taverns with a rich history of pulverizing livers.

YE OLDE CHESHIRE CHEESE

Known for: Dickens' fav

You know anything that's called "Ye Olde" is going to be ye good. This spot first served as a monastery in the thirteenth century and opened its tavernous doors as a pub in 1538. After getting caught up in the flames of the Great Fire of London, it was rebuilt in 1667 into its current iteration—which is a step into the far past with a roaring fireplace, cozy cellar, and creaking floorboards that have absorbed the heavy footsteps of Charles Dickens and Mark Twain.

THE OLD BANK OF ENGLAND

Known for: Sweeney Todd's butchery bar

With its muraled walls and chandeliered ceilings, this bar's got that "so fancy it's scary" vibe, and for good reason: It is said

to sit in the connecting space between Sweeney Todd's barbershop and Mrs. Lovett's pie shop. If you're not familiar, here's the gist: Todd was a psycho barber with sharp objects and Lovett made meat pies. A little snip here, a little trim there, and Todd's clients turned into Lovett's pies pretty quick. Our advice? Drink something strong and don't let anyone near your hair.

THE LAMB AND FLAG

Known for: famous fights

Established in 1772, this alleyway bar quickly became the place locals went to get drunk and beat the shit out of each other. The "Bucket of Blood"—as it was called back then because of its reputation for bare-knuckle boxing—is now pretty serene and covered in old photos of famous patrons. The upstairs room—named after poet John Dryden—is only accessed by a narrow, winding wooden staircase that'll give you a nice beating if you're not careful.

CITTIE OF YORKE

Known for: fantastic fireplace

If you're pissed off about the way Brits spell color and favorite, here's another one to gripe about. Cittie of Yorke is a step back into time, where furniture was wooden and creaky and people gathered around the unique fireplace made so that smoke goes down instead of up—to sip their liquor slow. To get a feel of the place,

order a drink from each of its three bars, especially the dank one down in the cellar. We promise that after a few drinks at Cittie, that language asshole inside your soul will get over it.

THE HOPE AND ANCHOR
Known for: punk past
The Hope and Anchor is a bar with a famous stage; everyone from the Sex Pistols to the Cure to the Pogues played their punk tunes to drunken Brits here. In the '70s, the Hope and Anchor was on the verge of being shut down until then-owner John Eichler came up with the brilliant plan of throwing shows featuring the best bands of the time. Knocking back a few at this bar will make you want to throw on your best spiky leather jacket, rip up your striped tights, fan out your Mohawk, and imagine rocking the fuck out to the Ramones (who have also played here).

OTP Tip: If secret cocktail bars stir your fancy, check out 5CC, a group of underground dark lounges scattered around London inside or beneath existing bars.

MOROCCO

WHAT THE F*CK IS KIF?

Morocco has long been a hotbed for spice markets, but they're also into another herb of sorts, and make a decent killing slinging it around the world. Usually smoked in combination with tobacco, Kif is hashish, a sticky brown brick of condensed marijuana. Moroccans love this lung-clouding "perfect bliss" (the direct Arabic translation), and if you've ever smoked the stuff, that translation couldn't be more spot on.

URBAN DICTIONARY

If you feel that any problem can be fixed by smoking weed and kicking around a hacky sack, then this kif's for you. In the interest of helping you look scholarly in front of your beanie-wearing, dread-head friends, let's upgrade your stoner dictionary. Ever heard of "50s" or "aces?" They're a half-cigarette, half-joint creation that some stoner undoubtedly concocted when he was short on the pot supply. Now add a "splif" of kif to your vocabulary: a concentrated mixture of pot rolled up with tobacco in a cigarette paper for your portable, mind-altering enjoyment.

HISTORY 101

In the early 1900s, kif was openly sold in Moroccan markets. It was sold as pure marijuana then, but in the '60s, English hippies swooped in and started mixing it with tobacco, creating the version we all know and love today. Kif has an interesting identity around the world. The uptight French have banned it, but it's perfectly legal in Spain. And in Morocco, although it's not a lawful activity, it's a popular one. Many young Moroccan boys start smoking at the age of nine or ten; we're jealous, as elementary school assemblies and times tables would have been way more fun after a couple of hits.

BUYERS BEWARE

Finding a kif dealer is like finding dirty sheets in a college dorm. While there's a dealer everywhere you look, buying kif from a stranger in public is a common rookie mistake. Sure, it seems convenient at the time, but the likelihood of finding out that said stranger is a police informant is quite high, and you'll end up in a dingy Moroccan prison without food, water, or your dignity. Despite being a chief export for Morocco and a major pastime for the male population, kif is actually illegal. If your idea of fun doesn't involve rubber gloves, a fistful of sand, and your tender parts, then you're better off getting the ingredients for your high elsewhere.

THE GOOD STUFF

Now, if you are a bong-toking tripper who came all the way to Morocco to find the kind, listen up. There isn't an eighth of Moroccan kif that comes with a money-back guarantee, so avoid purchasing last year's oregano by keeping your shopping away from street dealers. If you're friendly and outgoing, find a group of men in a café to discreetly smoke with and you can be fairly confident that the kif is of decent quality. Souvenir shoppers should look for small pipes called sebsis, or water pipes called hookahs (or hubbly bubblies) in

markets around Morocco. They won't be out on display, but can be found if you cruise into smaller bazaars. Keep your wits about you, and your personal belongings close to the vest when participating in illicit kif activity in Morocco.

OTP Tip: Remember that homegrown, Moroccan kif is going to be much more potent than the stuff your band-mate hid in your guitar case when you were crossing the Canadian border. Portion accordingly.

. . . AND THEY'RE ALWAYS GLAD YOU CAME

Nearly all of the kif in Morocco comes from the Rif Mountains that stretch from the Mediterranean Sea to the port city of Tangier. The police know the route all too well, so it's not wise to travel with kif anywhere in the country, as cops are looking to shake down hazy-eyed tourists. While you can get ten years in the slammer for buying or smoking kif in Morocco, not every square inch of Morocco is a kif land-mine. Chefchaouen is a chill spot where most people feel safe enough to puff the good stuff with their new-found homies in hostels and guesthouses. For a change up, try taking your toking to the beach or out into nature where the public won't be made to watch your high-as-a-kite shenanigans. You can let down your hair, dance around with tambourines, and take an irie look at a country that's a total mind-fuck with or without kif.

PARIS

CHEAP DILDOS AND FANCY-ASS SEX SHOPS

Baguettes aren't the only phallic objects you'll find in Paris. Don't let a TSA confiscation ruin your good times. Let OTP guide you to the finest sex shops in Paris to restock your toys and trinkets so you can leave squealing *"oui, oui"* all the way home.

DARK ALLEYS

If Ron Jeremy and Jenna Jameson were to marry, their reception would look something like Pigalle Place. During World War II, soldiers nicknamed the red light district "Pig Alley," as many would rabidly visit for a taste of the good stuff after months of celibacy at the barracks. Today, the area is still a sty—where people flock to buy sex toys like pigs to shit. Pick your pleasure with an assortment of toys, peep shows, strip clubs, and other X-rated attractions.

GET IN ON THE PDA

Paris is packed with enough sightseeing to *le puke*, and the Seine River is notorious for being Paris's most make-out-worthy attraction. Littered with beautiful bridges that offer unmatchable, multiperspective views of the city, this river comes with a live, busker-generated soundtrack to accompany your shameless groping. Hang out on the Pont Neuf and pack a picnic afterward for the Square du Vert-Galant. Then, park your lazy ass on one of the benches on the Pont des Arts; treat your eyes to the surrounding sights of the Eiffel Tower, the Louvre, and Notre Dame Cathedral; and start doing some slimy tongue push-ups.

TOUR DE FRANCE

Start your sexploits by visiting the Musée de l'Érotisme (Museum of Eroticism) at 72 Boulevard de Clichy. Floors one and two

are kinky paradise. Here, you can also find various figurines engaging in wild figurine sex, including tiny depictions of priests and nuns doing the nasty. The remaining floors house temporary exhibitions. After soaking up the museum culture, head to Rebecca Rils just down the street at 76-78. This *supermarché érotique* is a mainstream sex supermarket and attracts tourists (like your parents, which would be really awkward). The massive store is divided into four sections: DVDs, lingerie, gadgets, and shoes. The supermarché is great for basics like colorful furry handcuffs, masks, whips, nipple clamps, and chocolate sauce. For raunchier merchandise, visit Sexodrome at 23 Boulevard de Clichy. The 'drome is an adults-only Toys "R" Us, with more than 2,500 square meters of sex toys and apparatuses, freak-nasty reading material, and general filth.

THAT'S THE SPOT

As you walk up the stairs in the middle of the Boulevard de Clichy, you'll know you hit the right spot when it starts to smell like the Playboy mansion grotto after an all-night pool party. This den of sex is located directly below the Sacré Coeur Catholic church, perfect for cleansing your Catholic guilt or, more important, since Sacré Coeur sits at the highest point in Paris, checking

out the amazing views while testing out your recent purchases.

Paris may be known as the city of love, but it's got more than a few kinks down at the core. Let go of the sophistication front for a bit and let Pigalle stroke your libido in every which way.

DOING CRAZY-ASS TRIBAL DRUGS IN THE AMAZON

This isn't your everyday hallucinogen. But if those aren't cutting it anymore, up the psychedelic ante and venture into the mysterious world of *ayahuasca*. Native to Amazonian tribes, locals consider ayahuasca a medicine (don't call it a drug) that allows them to transcend a multidimensional universe, encounter demons from their past that live within, purge them from their bodies, and ultimately arrive in an unprecedented state of nirvana. Sound intense? That's because it is. And that's just the beginning. This is no poppable happy little party pill to make your nightmares go away so you can stop sleeping in your parents' bed. Ayahuasca, which means "vine of the soul" in Quecha is a sludgy, brown, gag-reflex inducing combination of the ayahuasca vine and chacruna leaves. One user described the taste as "Baileys Irish Cream mixed with prune juice." Let's get you all sauced up.

THE FACTS

For You Science Nerds

Neither the ayahuasca or chacruna plant on its own produces the mind and body trip for which ayahuasca is famous. According to the Western medicine explanation, the chacruna leaves contain the hallucinogen DMT. But our body contains monoamine oxidase (MAO), which destroys tryptamines such as DMT before they can be absorbed. However, the ayahuasca vine contains harmala alkaloids, which act as MAO inhibitors and allow the DMT to be absorbed in our blood stream and the hallucinations to begin.

For Us Regular People

Now, let's translate all of that to English. The chacruna plant has DMT, which is the awesome college dorm room party just waiting to happen. MAO, which is in our bodies, is the lame-ass RA next door who will write you up as soon as the noise gets above library-loud. The ayahuasca vine is an MAO inhibitor—the clever roommate who just baked the RA a sedative-laden apple pie. Let the DMT party commence.

WHAT IT FEELS LIKE

Endless, inescapable darkness surrounds you. Evil spirits circle like vultures in the distance, taking turns darting through you and tearing off a piece of your soul. One stops and pierces you with its stare. Transfixed by the fiery red eyes glowing from its skull, you hear a dark whisper. "You are trapped here. Forever." Its mouth does not move, but its eyes flare with every syllable like gasoline on a fire. You scream out to your shaman, who calmly walks over. "Está bien," you hear, followed by the ruffling of leaves and the massaging sound of spirit songs. The skull is sucked away like a vacuum into the abyss. Feeling returns to your extremities, and you are again in your own body. You open your eyes and see your shaman holding a small branch and sitting cross-legged next to you. His eyes, flickering in the candlelight, are a warm blanket on a cool summer night. The entire episode overwhelms you, and you roll over to vomit violently into the bucket next to your mat.

WHERE THE MAGIC HAPPENS

While the practice has gained a following in the States (especially Northern California), true ayahuasca rituals occur deep in the Amazon jungle and last for several days. It's a spiritual retreat, not a nightclub or rave. The ceremonies are led by master shamans, who spend years apprenticing under elder shamans to earn the coveted title. The curriculum includes learning the healing properties of various plants, navigating alternate realms, learning "spirit songs" to guide retreatants, and drinking enough ayahuasca to make Charlie Sheen say, "no, thanks." Shamans have been wandering other dimensions since before Jesus walked on water, although no one knows who was first responsible for this crazy concoction. Ceremonies take place at night in a quiet candlelit jungle lodge. When the ayahuasca is dispersed, the retreatants choke down the sludge, each with their own specific recipe and quantity, and the trip begins. Many call it the worst experience of their life: unforgiving darkness, suppressed emotions, and fear manifest as evil spirits and voices; visions of hell and the devil himself; and endless terror and misery. Buckets are provided to handle the inevitable vomiting.

THAT SOUNDS LIKE AWFUL BULLSHIT

Don't paddle away yet—there's a payoff. The shamans say confronting and defeating these evil spirits within us is the only way to absolve our souls of their existence. A cultish—yet sizable—following of people

agree and attribute ayahuasca to curing everything from depression to cancer. One such user says ayahuasca launches you to a reality you've never seen or even imagined, as opposed to the likes of acid and mushrooms, which only mind-fuck the world around you. "Other-worldly" is a pretty universal description among those that have braved the ordeal. The shamans say the vomiting is the embodiment of our purged demons. The trip lasts roughly six hours, but our pedestrian concept of time really has no meaning when realm-trotting. It may take several sessions, but once the internal demons are defeated and the darkness is broken, vivid heavenly visuals accompany a serene state of bliss. This follows the user back to our linear universe, where he is vindicated from a lifetime's worth of suppressed fear and despair.

YOUR PIECE OF PUKEY ENLIGHTENMENT

Iquitos, Peru, is the unofficial capital of ayahuasca tourism. At the airport, people will scream "ayahuasca" at you as you step outside, but do your homework beforehand and find a recommended master shaman. When you are transcending dimensions and plunging to the depths of inner hell, it helps to have a good tour guide.

WHAT THE F*CK IS A BOTELLÓN?

Bar in the car, BYOB, or a hidden flask full of the strong sauce—we've all got our own budget boozing tactics. But throw in a little good weather, some strapped-for-cash youth, and a culture that likes to knock 'em back, and you've got yourself the ultimate outdoor bender: *botellón*. Where do you sign up?

THE ORIGIN

The south of Spain might be known for those stupidly hot flamenco dancers, but one of the best things to come out of the region is botellón. Literally translated as "big bottle," botellón and all its trashy glory came to life in the '80s, when small groups of working-class locals would gather in plazas to get tipsy for cheap. Given Spain's love affair with the fiesta, it's no surprise that the tradition spread through the country like herpes during freshman year. Now, younger Spaniards toast (over and over again) to drinking and socializing without breaking the bank. We agree—it's the levelheaded thing to do.

BINGING LOGISTICS

Come weekend time, from 11:00 p.m. to as late as 3:30 a.m., Spanish plazas, parks, and alleys fill with fourteen- to almost-thirty-year-olds looking to binge on a budget before heading to more expensive bars and clubs. Say what? Yeah, in the land of the eighteen-year-old drinking age and living in casa till you tie the knot, parents just don't keep tabs on their teens like they do back home. And rather than drinking until their feet are numb, the Spaniards traditionally tend to keep their shit a tad more under control.

BRING IT

The bottled beverages at *botellón* vary, but like many important things in life, size matters. Often called *ir de litros*, or "to go out for liters," large quantities are the name of the game—from beer to juice mixtures and every other absurd fusion under the scorching Spanish sun. Most famous are the *kalimotxos*—a Basque beverage of mixology genius, which combines cola and dirt-cheap

red wine. The gnarly blend might not sound like a match made in heaven, but it handily shortens the distance between sober and drunk without your going bankrupt.

OTP Tip: Should you run out of drinks past purchase hours, keep an eye out for the lingering foreign street vendors hawking emergency *cervezas*.

BOTELLÓN HOTSPOTS

If you put a tracking device on any shitty bottle (or box) of Spanish alcohol, it would lead you to impromptu booze sessions taking place on university campuses across the country. Other hotspots include the Plaza del Carmen in Barcelona and plazas throughout the La Latina, Chueca, and Malasaña neighborhoods of Madrid. But really, come Thursday night, all squares, beaches, and parks are fair game.

OTP Tip: Macrobotellón is when people text and e-mail groups across the country to meet. This turns into a swarm of drinking and saliva-exchanging. When getting smashed at bars and *discotecas* starts to lose its luster—or when the money well runs dry—hit the streets with the Spanish teens. Bring your big bottle and make yourself at home—things are gonna get *muy* sloppy.

THE ELEPHANT MAN

Barcelona, Spain

If you happen to be trolling Barcelona for some booty, keep an eye out for this guy. Nobody knows his name, origin, or intentions, but anyone who's taken a trip to Barcelona has probably witnessed this old guy and his foot-long flaccid cockzilla freely flapping around town. He's permanently "dressed" with an underwear tattoo–a not-so-subtle "fuck you" to public nudity laws. Catch him chatting with cops, sippin' brews, posing for pictures, ramblin' down Las Ramblas, and simply hanging out.

PART 2

GET YOUR SHIT TOGETHER

Spontaneity is the beauty of backpacking, but to maximize your time, money, and experience abroad, you must first put in a little planning legwork. This section sorts out everything you need to know about getting your shit together to make the most of your trip. You'll need to figure out where you're going and for how long; construct a budget (and loosely stick to it); book the flight; and pin down some initial sleeping arrangements. From there, you'll get your backpack, necessary docs, and vaccines. To make this process easier, we've laid out the practical essentials and added some useful tips to get you the fuck out of here as fast as possible.

PLANNING
AND RESEARCH

So you've decided to leave it all behind and embark on a journey to discover the world (and yourself in the process). Now what? You may have a few destinations in mind, and doing your research before you leave will smooth out some of the bumps in the road. The planning stage is exciting, inspiring, and may save you some money, time, and heartache come liftoff.

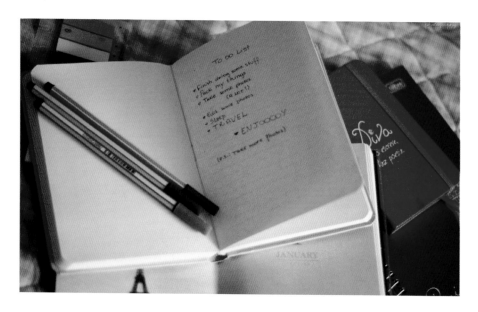

PLANNING

CHOOSING DESTINATIONS

Go where you've longed to see and keep your areas of interest in mind!

Europe has always been the foremost popular destination for backpackers. It's rich in culture, easy to navigate, and has a ton of photo opportunities—and, of course, many sexy Europeans. But, because Europe is not the cheapest destination, you may have to cut your traveling time or spend more time in cheaper countries (Moldova, Romania, Albania, and Bulgaria, to name a few) to make up for the difference. To maximize the time you can afford to travel, check out Southeast Asia and Central or South America. These places are extremely affordable, generally safe, and full of off-track adventures, parties, and hedonistic pleasures.

Questions to ask yourself when planning which country(ies) you want to explore:
+ Beaches or mountains? Need both?
+ Sunshine or clouds?
+ Cities or countryside?
+ English speakers or not?
+ Foodie destination or whatever you can eat out of a can?
+ Trains (do you need a rail pass?) or planes? Buses or cars? Boats?
+ Culture (museums, etc.) or outdoors/sports?
+ Multiple countries or just one?
+ Really safe or a little danger?
+ Drink or dry? (If your alcoholic tendencies need to be fed, avoid strict Muslim nations and places where the booze is stupid expensive. Or, use it as an opportunity to detox.)
+ Stretch your money or empty your wallet?
+ Love festivals/concerts or loathe 'em?
+ Loads of tourists or tourists are the plague?
+ Drugs mandatory or sobriety preferred?

Once you've narrowed down what you need, start looking for places that fit your criteria. Keep these tips in mind when you're chiseling out your itinerary:
+ You will most likely plan more activities and destinations than are realistically possible. Once you start traveling, you'll find that some destinations consume more or less time than what you originally imagined. Remember to check train or bus times between destinations, if that's how you're traveling. The journey between two cities can take an entire day or sometimes more, depending on where you want to go.
+ The beauty of backpacking is that you can choose to stay or leave whenever you want. You might even end up traveling with other backpackers you meet along the way. Set up some definite key places to visit and keep other plans flexible.
+ You'll be coming across many websites you will want to revisit. Set up a bookmark folder in your browser and save all the websites you find helpful, then merge them to your phone for safekeeping while on the road. HERE Maps is an app that saves your bookmarks

offline and hooks you up with turn-by-turn directions when you're Wi-Fi-less.

✈ Pinterest and Instagram are great resources for inspiration to keep track of your favorite destinations. Just follow relevant boards/feeds and let your mind wander to far-off places until your body follows.

CLIMATE AND SEASONS

Better weather means you will be competing with bigger crowds and dealing with things being more expensive. Although there could be more action in the midst of tourist madness, it's not a bad idea to hit the "shoulder" seasons, which are just before and just after the "high" season. You'll enjoy cheaper prices, flexible booking arrangements, and a better cultural experience. One small downside is you will likely have to pack for harsher weather. Climates vary dramatically around the world. A good example: Whether it's the rainy season (summer) or the dry season (winter), in some places, the temperature always stays hot or warm. So packing for a winter in Thailand is substantially different than packing for winter in Russia. Also, keep in mind that seasons are opposite above and below the equator—the United States celebrates Christmas when Australia hits the peak of summer. The cherry on top is global warming, which will throw some surprises your way too.

FESTIVALS, HOLIDAYS, AND EVENTS

If you plan to attend any festivals or big events, be sure to make your reservations (including transportation and accommodations to and from your festival destination) way in advance. For example, Oktoberfest in Munich attracts a giant tourist crowd (it's also a misnomer and actually occurs mostly in September). Tents should be reserved months in advance, as should hostels and couches. Do your research to find what, where, and when things go down. Merchants will often jack up prices of food and accommodations during festivals, so be sure to budget for the overage. During Oktoberfest, for example, hostels are often 300 to 500 percent more expensive.

LANGUAGE BARRIER

Prepare for some shocking news . . . Not everyone in the world speaks English! It's crazy, but it's true. You may actually find yourself in a place where *no one* will speak English. Don't freak out. First off, the best way to learn a language is to immerse yourself in it. You won't have to go out and spend $600 on Rosetta Stone just yet. Although coming to a country speaking a second language will definitely broaden your experience, communicating with people who don't speak your language becomes part of the adventure. Most people will try to help you, but it is essential that you learn the very basics before you go to any country (for general safety, and to show the locals that you're not arrogant and you're trying). If you're looking to study a new language abroad intensely, Transitions Abroad offers many worldwide language courses and programs. Learn more about studying abroad in Part 3: Make Yourself Useful (page 199).

POLITICAL CLIMATE

The United States and our media sometimes embellish the unsafe conditions and extent of political dilemmas present in foreign countries. Be sure to read about the safety conditions and political climates of the countries you plan to visit, but don't be discouraged from visiting destinations the United States advises against. If necessary, take it a step further and do some cross-referencing with the travel advisories

Don't forget, too, that if you're going to a place that has some tensions, political climates can change in an instant. Bone up on the Arab Spring of 2011 for an example of how governments can sink overnight. Staying on top of foreign events will give you an idea of what to expect. Read the free online articles from the *Economist*, Al Jazeera, and BBC for news outside the United States.

of other places like the UK and Australia.

Common sense and taking normal precautions will get you by in most places. Wikitravel.org's "Stay Safe" sections are usually written by locals or experienced travelers to that area; it's generally a good place to begin to get a valid idea of how dangerous a place really is.

OTP Tip: A great way to learn about foreign political and safety issues is by talking to locals and recent travelers directly. Follow Twitter feeds of locals who live in the places you want to go, particularly if it looks like the situation might be getting heated.

CULTURE SHOCK

Feeling overwhelmed and "hating" things, calling an experience or a food "weird," and/or generally wishing you were back home are all pretty telltale signs of culture shock. One of the best ways to avoid it is to get rid of expectations and prep yourself by reading up on the realities of what you'll face. Here are a few of the most common things that can cause people to experience culture shock.

THE THRONE

You've been on a hot bus all day long with the windows closed. Everyone is smoking. You're pressed up against a guy with two

chickens in his lap. Every bump reminds you that you've needed to pee for the last four hours. You finally stumble out of the bus and find the "bathroom": a plate (that's definitely been used) in the middle of a dirt floor. You cry, and then use it anyway, cursing this godforsaken country. This is a common scenario—from Greece to Turkey to Cambodia to India—and it can cause some serious internal (and external) drama if you're unprepared.

Before you leave the comforts of your home throne (particularly if you're headed to a developing country), figure out the toilet situation in advance. Mental preparation is half the battle in avoiding culture shock.

GUIDE TO TOILETS AROUND THE WORLD

Sir Thomas Crapper, although not the inventor of the flush-toilet as popularly believed, was a hell of a guy. The pusher of potties, the bad boy of bathrooms, Crapper advocated the use and development of sanitary plumbing for his entire life. The world caught on quickly, and the use of toilets spread globally. Since the humble days of Crapper, people around the world have thought of new and interesting ways to drop off their smellies:

Germany–Poo Platform
Just like a mullet, this shitter is all about business in the front and party in the back. Upon flushing, water rushes out from the back and hypothetically washes your turds into the hole in the front. This interpretation of the toilet is quite counterintuitive, and some major flaws exist with this design. Mainly, the lack of a water barrier between your goods and the toilet creates a horrid preflush smell, and upon flushing, streakage is highly likely.

China–Squatters
These shit holes (very literally) evoke the image of communism. They are bare, rugged, and as it turns out, extremely intimidating to foreigners. There are countless squatter how-to guides that address the important issues, like the fear of falling in. Here is the only guide you will ever need: see a hole, pull down your pants, squat, and go.

England–The UriLift
The UriLift was invented to remedy the insane amount of drunk-man piss on the streets of England. Whether it fixes the problem or not, this thing kicks ass. During the day, it is hidden in the ground, and when the partying begins, it peeks its smelly head to the surface to service those drunk enough to not care that their bare asses are hanging out in the middle of the street.

Japan–Extreme High Tech
In Japan, your toilet situation is a total crapshoot. On any given visit, you may find yourself hovering over a hole in the ground (see China's squatters), or at the opposite extreme, you'll have remote-control arm rests that make your stay on the seat very enjoyable and luxurious. Using the high-tech toilet is like flying a space shuttle, with buttons for just about any bathroom predicament you may find yourself in. There's a noise button to mask the sound of whatever you need to do while in the john (yodeling for instance), one that activates a blow-dryer, a clock to time your visit (handy for when you're training for the logging event in the Bodily Functions Olympics), and more.

Russia–Seatless
In one of the coldest places in the world, it's wonderful to know that when you need to go and squatting is not your forte, your ass will probably freeze to the porcelain bowl, as no cushy plastic seat is attached. Furthermore, Russians consider toilet paper of any kind a luxury.

Brazil–Button Pushers
Whereas other toilets are preset to flush an average amount of cargo, this one leaves it in your hands. Equipped with a flush button, but no septic tank, your job is to hold the button down for a continual flush until you feel it's time to move on.

Australia–Counterclockwise
We don't understand the fascination with the counterclockwise flushing down under. (And who notices these things? You know who–people who stare down at the toilet after they're done. We caught you.) We don't care which direction it spins, as long as it goes down.

EATS

Nothing can derail a trip faster than a food meltdown. But before you park yourself at McDonald's to chow down on fries in an attempt to shake the shock, read up on the food culture of the country (or countries) you're headed to. You might need to make some dietary concessions, depending on where you are and what the locals serve. Learn ahead of time what the fare might be. If you're a picky eater, have religion-based food restrictions, are vegetarian/vegan, or have a severe food allergy (peanuts would be tough in Thailand, or a gluten allergy in Italy), you should plan ahead, knowing what foods you can and cannot eat, including the names in the local lingo. Also, foods that sound familiar might be completely different—in Spain, a tortilla is a potato omelet, not a burrito wrapper or taco shell.

Remember, food is part of the experience. There will be times when you order something seemingly harmless and a baked goat head with eyeballs will show up twenty minutes later. Roll with the punches, take a photo for Instagram, and chalk it up as part of the journey. It's all going down that culturally shocking shitter anyway.

SEX AND SEXES

Depending on where you go and which gender you happen to be, understand that you might have to bend to cultural norms. If you're female, for example, and covering yourself from head to toe in 110-degree weather sounds more like living in a slow cooker than having an adventure, avoid Zanzibar during Ramadan. Read up on dress styles and try and pack as close to the local attire as possible. Save a little money for buying appropriate clothing on the road, which will also make great souvenirs when you get back home.

Public displays of affection can get you jailed in some countries, and same-sex overtures can get you beaten or killed in others. Jamaica, for example, has a strong antigay culture that has been denounced for years by human rights groups. Don't wait to find out what the sexuality norms are in your destination. Spend some time learning about what's expected of you as a visitor. And don't forget to pack condoms, birth control, and/or Plan B-types of pills. These might not be readily available—or even legal to buy—where you're headed.

THREE FEET OF PERSONAL SPACE

While spending the bulk of an afternoon nuts deep in someone else's chili can be a consensual experience, when traveling, this scenario probably just means you're riding public transportation in a place where personal space is defined a bit differently (this is common in many parts of Asia). You'll know everything every stranger around you ate for dinner, and you'll smell the aroma of two weeks' worth of sweat that's been baked in the hot sun. Knowing the deal in advance will help you take a deep (mouth open, nose pinched) breath and tell yourself it's all good. Bring a hanky doused in lavender.

ANIMAL FARM

Animals aren't always treated equally, and if animal abuse breaks your heart so much that you can't bear to see it, there are a few places you might want to avoid. Do your due diligence and figure out what's going on with the animal situation where you're going. Understand, too, that what you feel strongly about probably won't resonate with the locals. Better to be prepared than to be surprised by puppies for sale . . . for dinner.

SOLO, PARTNER, OR GROUP?

SOLO

If this is your first time traveling abroad independently, seriously, go solo! We feel damn strongly about this assertion—even if not for the entirety of your trip, at least for a portion.

Why? Well, you will decide what *you* want to do, where to go, what you like, dislike, how long to stay, and when to leave. It is a time to learn about *you*! You will have more time to take photos, write in your journal, read, study, observe, and reflect. You will feel empowered to know you can survive on your own with very little in this big world. Freedom at last! You have the opportunity to meet many other travelers going solo and open yourself up to meeting locals and enriching your cultural experience. For you introverted types, you may find a whole new extroverted you.

Traveling solo may sound intimidating at first, but if you overcome the initial hesitation to go solo, the reward will be tenfold. If you are concerned about your safety going solo, check out our Health and Safety section (page 183) to learn how to protect yourself on all fronts.

TRAVEL PARTNERS

If you decide to travel with someone, you must closely examine the relationship you have with this person and whether it will withstand the added pressures of traveling. Some things to think about:

→ How well do you communicate problems?

→ Is your partner independent enough to allow you some alone time?

→ Does your partner have his/her own budget/funds?

+ Is your partner an experienced traveler?
+ Have you spent a prolonged period of time with this person in close quarters before?
+ How motivated is your partner to physically travel?
+ Does he/she snore? If yes, consider your threshold.
+ Is your travel partner really fun at parties? If so, is he/she fun because he/she is drunk and passed out? Consider how his or her social tendencies will play out when traveling.

If the answer to one or more of these questions about your travel buddy gives you pause, maybe it's time to find a new travel partner. (Better to know now rather than when you're sharing a tent halfway across the world.) Check online for sites that will connect you with like-minded peeps. But remember, you can always cut out the headache by traveling solo.

TRAVELING IN GROUPS

You love your friends, so why not have a great time together all around the world? Additionally, traveling en masse might come with the benefits of group rates and split costs. First though, consider the following:
+ People bitch. When everyone wants to do the same thing, at the same time, for the same duration, at the same price, traveling in a group is beautiful. Sadly, unless you're all clones of each other, there is no way everyone will always agree on everything. Fights will break out over stupid nonissues and miscommunications.
+ People get sick. Some people are whiny when they're sick, and you will have to deal with them dragging you down until they're better.
+ People are late. When one person is late, everyone is held up. Enjoying your group rate will be impossible if you miss the flight, for example.
+ People smell. One more smell other than your own can be doable; five more smells and you're in nausea territory.

The bigger the group, the more issues you may have to deal with. Obviously, it's not impossible to have a great trip as a group, but you will have to compromise your own idea of the perfect trip to incorporate the wants, needs, and quirks of everyone you choose to travel with. If you love your friends more than your sanity, there are several websites that have a good handle on setting up group travel rates at discount prices, STA (STATravel.com).

TECHNOLOGY: THERE'S AN APP FOR THAT

Prepping for your trip isn't just about where to go and what to pack. These days it also includes making sure your technology goes with you. Sure, there are still places on this planet where you'll find yourself in Internet cafés or where the interwebs haven't arrived—and yes, we recommend going there too!—but most of us are digitally dependent. Here are a few apps to download before you hit the road to keep you from getting derailed.

TripAdvisor/Yelp
There's something to be said for finding restaurants, hotels, and attractions without relentless research, but sometimes you just want someone to tell you if it's infested with cockroaches. TripAdvisor attracts an older crowd of curmudgeons while Yelp (which recently went global) serves the younger complaining types.

Hipmunk
An airline search engine that allows you to filter the search based on more specific variables than just your departure and arrival cities, such as "agony" (e.g., if you're trying to avoid a three-day layover in Jaipur on your way from Frankfurt to Bucharest).

SkyScanner
This app works great for booking budget international flights. You can leave the destination field open and it'll tell you the cheapest places to fly from wherever you are.

Google Flights
A fare tracker app—use it to find the cheapest flights.

Tripit
Integrates with your calendar and Facebook, and will forward your itinerary to Mom and Dad (or whomever else you want) so they know where you are in space and time.

Packing Pro
For all you list-making types, this will help you keep your shit organized so you won't forget the essentials (like your passport).

Postcard Star
Send your badass photos back home on a postcard. You take a pic; you type your greeting; and then Postcard Star prints and sends it. Bam. Done.

GUIDEBOOKS, BLOGS, AND TRAVEL AGENCIES

Guidebooks are still a great source of information for making your travel plans. But with a barrage of travel blogs now all over the Internet, you can find amazing and current insight and advice posted by travel writers who are out traveling your preferred destination right now—so start Googling! Following Twitter feeds of your favorite travelers, expats, and travel sites (@offtrackplanet, in case you were wondering) is also a great way to get inspired and gather intel for your trip.

GUIDEBOOKS

Skim through *Rough Guides*, *Footprint*, *Let's Go*, and *Lonely Planet* books and compare the different publications to see which fits your style best.

+ Make sure to check the publication date of the book.
+ Unless you intend to spend the majority of your time in one single country, get a book that focuses on an entire continent (or broad region).
+ If you do intend to buy books, and you've picked out the ones you like, buy them online! You can save up to 85 percent buying used books through Amazon or Half.com. Instead of bringing your massive guidebook (which will occupy prime real estate in your backpack and make you look like a douche), tear out the pages you need, staple them together, and stick it in your travel journal.
+ Don't forget the apps. These days, a lot of travel guides have free or cheap apps for your country of choice.

TRAVEL AGENTS AND TOUR GUIDES

Travel Agents

These guys take on the task of discount hunting for your travel needs. In many countries, taking a gap year (a year off to travel before moving on to college or work) is popular, and some travel agencies cater

specifically to the gap year crowd. Using these guys can result in some killer deals for eighteen- to twenty-five-year-olds.

The United Kingdom (a gap year country) has some good sites, so include "UK" as a keyword in your searches. Unfortunately, travel agencies in the United States generally cater to an older, less "backpack-y" traveling crowd. (Yes, we think this sucks too . . . we're working on it.) For the most part, agents will try to sell you prepackaged guide tours, which are boring and a cop-out to real backpacking. One agency that comes close to understanding the needs of backpackers is STA Travel, who generally caters to people twenty-five and under.

Tour Guide Packages

Packaged tour guides provide you with a choice of itineraries that are full of popular travel destinations and activities. You'll have a built-in group of travel companions, and you won't have to worry about the details. This might be the right decision for some, but this also *defeats the purpose of independent travel.* It's touristy as hell, and, just like your trip, your travel stories will be bland and prepackaged. But, if you're into that kind of thing, check out Intrepid Travel and Contiki.

Finally, don't stress out too much about trying to figure everything out all at once. One of the most valuable things you'll learn from your traveling experience is how adaptable you are. In fact, you might even miss the point if you stay completely within all your plans. This is a journey enhanced by learning to change direction or by getting a bit . . . fuck it, at the risk of sounding cheesy, *off track!*

PASSPORT

PASSPORTS AND VISAS

In order to leave this country, you'll need a passport. Some countries also require visas for entrance or to work, study, or stick around a while. This is step one to get you off your ass and into the world. We've been there and have the rashes to prove it, so here is what you need to get started.

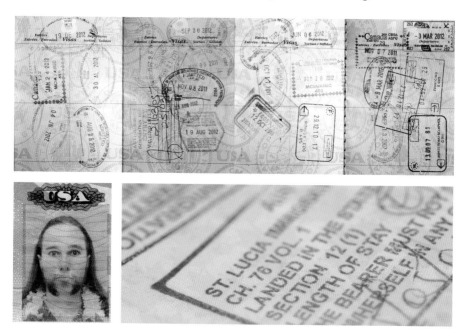

PASSPORTS

TRAVEL.STATE.GOV

This US Department of State website is something our government has actually done right. It has well-organized, complete, and official information regarding passports, visas, embassies, and guidelines for visiting every country on the planet. You should visit this website early and often when planning any international trip.

PASSPORT

Your ticket to the world—any US citizen can get a passport. Here's how:

1. Dig up your proof of citizenship (birth certificate, previous passport, or certificate of citizenship) and your driver's license or state ID.
2. Make a copy, front and back, of both forms of ID.
3. Get one passport picture at any drugstore with a photo department in five minutes for about $10. Take off your glasses; don't wear a hat or bling; and don't smile. No duck faces, and keep your shirt on.
4. Go to Travel.state.gov/passport/ and fill out the DS-11 form online. Print it out.
5. Submit your application at a post office or municipal government office.

Routine processing for a passport takes four to six weeks and costs $110 (plus $25 for first-timers). Expedited processing is two to four weeks and will run you an extra $60. If you're traveling within two weeks or need to get a visa within four, it will cost extra, but you can schedule an appointment at one of the twenty-five government passport agencies, and they'll hook you up with a little blue book faster.

PASSPORT CARD

A passport card can be used to travel to Mexico, Canada, or the Caribbean by land or sea (not air!). The application process is about the same as for a passport book, but it fits in your wallet and is $80 cheaper. It's handy if you live near a border and cross it often, but for the type of travel you should be doing, you'll need a passport book.

HOW TO HANDLE YOUR PASSPORT

→ *Don't lose it!* Take plenty of precautions. Don't walk around with your passport (unless the country you're in requires you to have it at all times). Instead, carry a copy of your passport and visa (if there is one) in your wallet, stash one in your bag, and give one to a travel buddy. Also, e-mail a copy of your passport and visas to yourself in case you lose all your shit and need to prove to Uncle Sam at an embassy that you are family.

→ *If you do lose it* . . . US passports let you move rather easily around most of the world (good news), so the black market for them is huge (bad news). If it gets lost or stolen, go to the nearest US embassy. They will wipe your tears and get you a replacement ASAP.

WHO'S YOUR DADDY? WHAT THE US EMBASSY CAN DO FOR YOU

Who *Are* These Guys?

A US embassy is the headquarters for US affairs in a foreign country and assists and protects the rights of Americans in that country. Embassies are in most foreign capital cities, and consulates (basically a junior embassy) are in many other major cities. Both are there to help you when you're screwed.

The STEP Program

Relax, we're not sending you to rehab (yet). STEP (Smart Traveler Enrollment Program) is provided for free by the government to assist you abroad in case of an emergency and to send you routine info or travel advisories from certain embassies. It takes just a few minutes to set up an account at Step.state.gov and register your upcoming trips. So do it.

What the US Embassy *Can* Do

If you lose your passport, the embassy will whip you up an emergency one in no time. If you need medical help, they can direct you to some good local docs or help arrange a return to the States, if needed. If you get robbed, they can tell you where to file a police report and help you get money from home if you lose everything. If you're completely SOL, they may even give you a loan to get back to the States.

What the US Embassy *Can't* Do

If you fuck up and get thrown in some dingy foreign slammer, the US embassy will not send in SEAL Team Six to whisk you away to safety. You're expected to abide by the laws of the country you are in, even if those laws are different than back home. So if you get busted committing international atrocities such as gum chewing in Singapore or PDA in Dubai, don't expect Uncle Sam to bail you out.

What If I Am Arrested?

You may not get your one phone call, but foreign law enforcement should let you contact your embassy, which can point you to a local lawyer, contact your one cool uncle for bail money, and make sure you are treated humanely according to international law. Unless you indicate otherwise, the embassy must legally keep any info about you private, so Mommy never has to know you were caught with a poppy seed bagel in Singapore (because that's illegal!).

When Shit Really Hits the Fan

If a military coup is threatening to disrupt your hammock time, make sure you are registered with the local embassy through STEP and follow the suggestions in e-mails or news reports. If shit gets bad, they may recommend you leave the country. If shit gets really bad and commercial travel isn't safe, they may even coordinate an evacuation.

A visa is a document or stamp placed in your passport that acts as an endorsement to enter a country. Many countries require a visa for entrance, and most do for work, study, or extended stays. Some you can get at the border (or when you arrive), and others you need to obtain in advance. Specifications and requirements can vary widely—for most places in Europe you don't even need one. If you're looking for a visa to trek around places not in the EU, however, you'll need to take a look at their visa requirements. Once again, Travel.state.gov will let you know all the specifics for entering a country, as well as where to go to get a visa, if needed. Plan ahead—some visas take weeks to get, and sometimes, if you don't have one, you'll be denied boarding on your flight or will be turned away at the border.

MONEY AND BUDGETING

If you've never traveled independently before, your primary concern may be cost-related—around $1,000 per month is a fair medium estimate for a backpacker's monthly budget. This estimate should keep you fed, clothed, and with a roof over your head in any country around the world. (Some places are cheaper than others, but you will be surprised at how much you can do on this small budget.) There are, of course, many other variables to consider, including pretrip expenses.

PRETRIP EXPENSES

Before you start planning your budget, you should have a little convo with yourself about what the word "budget" actually means to you. Staying true to broke-ass backpacker ideals by always choosing the cheapest option may take its toll after several months of sleeping on the ground for free and eating $2 street-meat. As such, factoring in a little cash to treat yourself to a nice room and a sit-down meal may be something to think about. Keepin' it real with yourself about how low you're willing to go is essential in determining how much money you'll need once you get to your destination. Just remember the old rule: Take half of your shit, twice the money, and you'll do fine. All prices discussed here are in USD.

BACKPACK
$120 to $300
Besides plane tickets, your backpack can be the most expensive purchase of the entire trip. Make sure to try on a bunch and do some comparative shopping before you say "I do" to the one you love. A backpack with a daypack can be worth the extra money. And, do yourself a favor: spend a few extra bucks on a lock—at the very least, it's $10 well spent to protect your big travel investment. (See page 176 for more on choosing the right pack.)

TRAVEL SUPPLIES/ TOILETRIES
$30 to $100
Although keeping your dirty parts clean is key, you don't need a bunch of eau-de-what-not products to do so. Buy a few basic travel-size items to get you started and remember that people all over the world get by just fine without $25 shampoo. Bringing a few items like aspirin and anti-diarrhea tablets along could be a lifesaver if you get the runs on the road and don't know where the local drugstore is.

VACCINATIONS
$0 to $300
You don't want your trip cut short by an incurable disease. So, once you decide where you want to go, check out the Centers for Disease Control website at Cdc.gov. Click on your destination country (or countries), and you'll find a list detailing all diseases present in that region and the vaccinations you'll need to get. Call around to several travel clinics and doctors to see whose stab rates are the lowest—and it's worth asking if you can bargain a price for a one-stop-shot. Don't put off getting stabbed until the last minute: some vaccines take up to eight weeks to start working their magic.

PASSPORT/VISA FEES
$0 to $250
Passports and visas are costs you cannot avoid. Certain countries require their own special visa, so factor that cost in as well. And you won't get very far across any border without a passport. Make sure that *all* of your documents are up to date, and make copies of and scan, then e-mail yourself all important papers before you leave.

DISCOUNT CARDS
$25 to $28

If you're a full-time student, buying an International Student Identity Card (ISIC) could save you much more than the price of the card itself (around $25). Having one of these cards gets you discounts on a variety of things, from museums to train tickets. If you're not a student and under twenty-six, you can apply for an International Youth Travel Card (IYTC), which gets you all the same benefits as the ISIC. For $28 you can become a member of Hostelling International and get discounts on hostel bookings, museum admissions, and travel services.

TRAVEL INSURANCE
$60 to $260

We get why some people would skip travel insurance to save a few bucks, but unless you plan on traveling in a bubble while wearing a padded suit, consider travel insurance a priority if you're visiting slightly sketchy places. The fact is that you never know what could happen—and while we're not trying to be your mother, we doubt you have an extra $10,000 to $100,000 lying around in case a major medical emergency happens. Travel insurance will also cover bag loss (or theft), and offers 24/7 phone support if the shit hits the fan.

TRANSPORTATION
$300 to $5,000

There are more websites to help you find cheap flights than there are airlines. But, remember to read the fine print of ticketing restrictions before you click "buy"—some sites will charge you a booking fee that can be avoided by going to the airline website directly. Factoring in all the costs of planes, trains, and automobiles can be tricky, so plan on overestimating just in case you want to splurge on a cab back to the hostel. Some hostels rent bikes for minimal fees, and nothing beats the price of walking.

Before you hit the road, make sure to find out the current exchange rate for the country you are visiting. We recommend consulting Xe.com to gauge how far you can stretch your dollar.

ACCOMMODATIONS
$0 to $60 per night

Consider hostels and Airbnb your new homes away from homes while traveling. Cheaper than even the most budget-friendly hotels, most hostels will sleep anywhere from two to twenty in a room (private rooms are available in most for more money) and will offer some of the best opportunities for meeting like-minded travelers, or hot, temporary bedmates. Depending on where you are traveling, the time of year, and exchange rates, the price of hostels can vary significantly. Airbnb rentals vary by type (you can rent just a room or entire home or apartment), location (out in the boonies or central downtown), and season. If paying $5 for a hostel bed seems like too much, check out Couchsurfing.org, where free is the way to be.

EATING/DRINKING
$10 to $30 per day

In general, this is a cost that varies according to how much you like to eat, how restrictive your dietary needs are, and how many drinks it takes you to get a sufficient buzz. In many countries, eatin' on the streets is the most authentic and least expensive way to grub. Finding a hostel with a kitchen can be a win-win situation that saves you cash and scores you ass. Everyone knows that the fastest way to any hottie's heart is through the stomach, so hit up the local market for some groceries and whip up a cheap meal that will impress the traveling tail.

SIGHTSEEING/MUSEUMS
$0 to $100 per week

While your nights may be filled with bars and clubs, your days will likely be filled with cultural activities. Decide which sights you are willing to pay to see and for which just snapping a pic and moving on will suffice. Staring at the Eiffel Tower from afar is free, while getting to the top will cost ya. Most museums will have one day of the month when they are free for all, so it's worth doing a little investigating before you plunk down a wad of cash on admission fees. Many museums will offer student discounts, while others will suggest a donation. With so much shit to see in every country, fees can add up quickly—skip some of the touristy places with pricey admissions in favor of smaller attractions. Everyone visits the Louvre in Paris, but how many can say they've been to the Musée des Vampires? Check out the first section of this book for quirky inspiration (starting on page 11).

PARTYING
$10 to $50 per week

Get your party started right by doing some pregamin' in the hostel. You can split the cost of a bottle with your hostel mates and play some international drinking games before heading out to save some cash you'd otherwise blow at the bar. Many hostels will have their own bar with cheap drink specials—and the added bonus of being close to your bed for those moments when you meet a "special friend."

COMMUNICATING
$5 per week

Outside of checking in with Moms and Pops to let them know how responsible you're being (wink, wink), your communication (and therefore your costs) can be kept to a bare minimum. You didn't travel across the world to be on the phone, so let people know you're alive with a quick e-mail. If you're dying to see the boyfriend you left behind, get some face-time for free via Skype. Or, you can add international call and text messaging to your phone plan for cheap. Remember that you can tell everyone about your trip for free when you get back.

LAUNDRY
$2 to $10 per week

Many hostels will have laundry facilities on-site for a small fee. If not, ask the front desk where the nearest coin-operated Laundromat is. Otherwise, buy a small box of detergent and make a sink your new washing machine—use your bedposts as an overnight air-dryer and you'll have a nice, clean pair of skivvies by the morning. The straps on your backpack also make a great dryer when times get rough—if you're on foot and it's warm out, loop a few things through your straps to give them some fresh-air time.

SOUVENIRS
$5 to $25

Bringing back a trinket from your trip can be a nice gesture to say, "I was somewhere cooler than you were." Steer clear of the tourist shops that will jack up all the prices on lame, touristy crap that no one wants. Instead, check out local flea markets or artist fairs to score one-of-a-kind tchotchkes and garb on the cheap. Saving your shopping until the last day or two will save you from hauling other people's shit all over the world with you.

MISCELLANEOUS
$20 per week

You want to have a little cushion money for things that may pop up that aren't necessarily essential expenses. For times when you find out about a concert or festival you're psyched about while on the road, you unexpectedly run out of shampoo because the chick you're hooking up with used it to wash her lion mane, you feel like tricking out your backpack with hydraulics, or whatever it may be, having a bit of extra spending money not reserved for anything in particular is nice. Just don't consider this a spike to your drinking budget, or you'll end up in the gutter, penniless.

FLIGHTS AND TRANSPORTATION

Buying that initial plane ticket out of the country can be hard on the wallet. Ticket prices vary widely from one continent to the next and within regions. A ticket to Paris is sometimes comparable in cost to a semester's tuition, but a flight from Paris to London can run you the price of a pack of Wrigley's (as in less than one euro; shocking but true). Here's the rundown on getting from point A to point B—with a bunch of sea in between.

Start your trip from the cheapest location in the United States possible. If you live in Bumblefuck, you're likely to save big by arranging transportation to a major international hub. This could mean volunteering to drive an old lady's car to Florida, taking a Greyhound to New York, or hopping a train to Houston, Chicago, or Dallas. Amtrak, Greyhound, Megabus, and car exchanges are surprisingly cheap ways to get around the States.

When booking from the big city, expand your horizons. Check Priceline, Travelocity, Momondo, Google Flights, SkyScanner, and Kayak, which are sites that compare several airlines and dates at once so that you can get a general idea of ticket prices. Keeping your dates flexible sets you up for finding the best rates possible. STA Travel is an old-school travel agency that has sixteen locations around the country, all close to college campuses. With a student ID, you can score a ticket at a price that will make businessmen jealous.

If you're heading out to do some good in the world, there are organizations that subsidize transportation. If you're set up to volunteer, check out FlyForGood.com and score a discount on airfare to the volunteer destination. Flip through our volunteer section (page 199) to get some ideas on how to go the good route.

Getting off-grid is great, but keeping that smartphone active could be helpful. There are a ton of apps that make travel smoother. FlightStats specializes in tracking flights, and GateGuru provides useful maps of sprawling international hubs. Delta has an app to track your luggage, which is helpful when everything you own is at the mercy of multiple airports.

TYPES OF TICKETS

Flights don't just come and go. There are several different types of airline tickets—some with more tricks up their sleeve than Amelia Earhart.

ROUND-TRIP

If you only have a short time, or if you're Captain Organized and have your route planned out, opt for a tried-and-true round-trip ticket. Choose a spot to bookend your travels, and plan to use local or regional transportation between destinations. A round-trip ticket can be reassuring, especially for travel virgins, because beginning and end dates are tangible. It can also be cheaper in the long run: a single-leg ticket to London, for example, is sometimes only slightly less than a round-trip one. Just keep in mind that once you do this, you're locked in.

GO AND DON'T COME BACK

If you've got more time on your hands or don't know exactly where you want to go, join the ranks of bank robbers and fugitives and book a seat one way. With a one-way ticket, you're as flexible as a yoga teacher. Say you're chilling with a group in Tangier that's headed to Dubai tomorrow, and you decide you want to tag along. With no return trip planned, you're free as a bird. Those palm-shaped islands are yours. Just be sure to set aside enough in your bank account to get home eventually—unless you're planning on pulling a Bonnie and Clyde.

OPEN-JAWS

These are multidestination tickets that make your trip a three-way. You'll still pick a place to bookend your travels, but you can also hit up a couple of spots in between. An open-jaw ticket typically goes from Point A to B to C and back to A. You'd be interested in one of these if you're trying to cover mad ground, or if long-distance trains and buses aren't your thing. They're also good if you're planning to travel for six months or more, because it gives your wandering a backbone and keeps aimless vagabonding tendencies in check.

AIRPASSES

Airpasses are promotional packages offered by allied airlines around the world. Each pass has a predetermined list of cities you can choose from, and the ticket price includes a stop in each city you choose. Residents of any city included are ineligible for an Airpass. You're sacrificing flexibility, but if you score a good deal, you can always tack on more time before or after your set itinerary.

AROUND THE WORLD (RTW)

An RTW ticket is like buying wholesale—each ticket included costs a little bit less than it would alone. Beginning at roughly $4,000, an RTW can be a lot to put out, but other than trying to paddle a raft around the globe for forty years, this is the cheapest way to see the world. Do your research; some include party fouls such as only being able to fly in one direction or having to book round-trips. Check out OneWorld.com, SkyTeam.com, and Star Alliance.com to get started.

JOIN THE MiLE-HIGH CLUB!

Just getting laid won't get you many high fives anymore. To join the truly elite lovers club, board a plane and engage in some freaky activity 40,000 feet above the ground. Here's how:

Get a Partner

Unless you're with someone you hump regularly, you'll need to scout out a partner. Don't be a boarding gate creeper, but hit up the nearest airport pub instead. Scan the bar for a boarding pass with the same flight, "randomly" grab a seat next to your target, and get to work.

Timing

Timing is key. On overnight flights, wait until everyone is asleep or watching Nicolas Cage ruin a movie. On shorter flights, wait for the drink service to start. The flight attendants are your mile-high cock blocks, so make sure they are distracted.

Make Your Move

Do your prep work at the seat and go *one at a time* to a predetermined bathroom. On the bigger overnight planes, the midcabin bathrooms are bigger, and flight attendants linger in the back all night. On daytime flights, the back bathrooms are your love lavs–out of sight from the rest of the cabin.

The Act

You're not here to set any marathon records, so no need to think of sports to prolong this one. Get in, and get out. Bring a rubber–you won't find condom dispensers in these bathrooms. When

you're done, walk to your seats separately and avoid eye contact. Either way, the deed is done, and no amount of shame can take away your membership card.

Congratulations to the newest inductees of the mile-high club. It's about time you stopped flying *Virgin*.

While our highways kick ass and the road trip is as American as apple pie, we're behind the times when it comes to getting around on the ground. Most parts of the world have elaborate train and bus systems that make Amtrak look like your toy set around the Christmas tree, and Greyhound look like a Chihuahua. There's no better way to understand the true essence of a country than by utilizing its mass-transit systems, and in most backpacker hot spots, mass transit is the fastest and most reliable way to get around.

EURAIL PASSES

European train trips are legendary—chances are if you've been to Europe, you've boarded one of these bad boys. Travel between European countries is more like crossing a state line, and the über-developed train system is your ticket to just about anywhere. If you're backpacking across Europe for a while, you should definitely consider getting a Eurail Pass.

Broken down by distance of travel, there are several different types of passes. The Global Pass includes all rail travel to and within twenty-eight countries. A Select Pass gives you access to four bordering countries of your choice (for instance France, Germany, Italy, and Spain) and a Regional Pass enables you to travel within and between two bordering countries. If you're planning on spending your whole sojourn getting spiritual with Greek goddesses or exercising your Italian stallion for a while, opt for a One Country Pass, where travel is unlimited within the country of choice. Tickets are cheaper the younger you are—snag a youth ticket (if you're twenty-five or under) for a 35 percent discount. If both you and your travel partner are twenty-six or older, the Small Group Saver will knock off 15 percent.

There are a handful of Eurail apps that will bring train schedules to your finger-tips, which can make all the difference in the world.

ASIAN TRAINS

Getting around China or India by car or bus ain't no European holiday. Heavy road traffic is caused by animals with the same right-of-way as rickshaws and enough peo-ple to clog the world's arteries. Metal bus seats and bumpy roads can leave your ass baboon-blue after a long trip. The best way to get around these giant countries is to train it. There are several different class lev-els, and they vary from country to country.

Train compartments hold up to six people, and overnight trains usually have a Sleeper Class. Opt for a top bunk if you're into personal space, because lower berths serve as benches during the daytime. A cramped General Class ticket is hardly worth the money you'll save. Most trains also have a more expensive A/C Sleeper Class, in which you'll find more privacy and less sweat.

BUSABOUT

Busabout, which operates throughout nine countries in Europe (and which has routes in Northern Africa), is comparable to Euro-rail in the way that it works. You'll be issued a pass based on your preferred destina-tions and length of travel. Busabout tickets, however, are specifically designed for backpackers, so bust out that booze and make some friends. There are adventure, trekking, festival-geared, and hop-on, hop-off options. Check out Busabout.com to create your own trip.

SOUTH AMERICAN BUSES

Nowhere in the world is there a more developed bus system than the interna-tional routes crisscrossing South America.

The quality of these buses depends on the wealth of your country of origin. Long-distance Argentine buses, for example, are usually double-decker, air-conditioned beauties with fully reclining seats and even free hot coffee. Buses in Bolivia or Ecuador are a lot rougher, but they've got character—and build it, too.

International pricing varies from country to country, but it's almost always cheaper than flying. You'll need to budget for Colombian buses, but the bus route running the gringo trail from La Paz to Cusco will hardly dent your wallet. Be sure to hit up the terminal ticket booth a day before you want to travel, and don't forget to ask if the bus has a bathroom on board.

REINVENTING THE ROAD TRIP

Rental cars are usually the most expen-sive mode of transport, but there's nothing quite like getting behind the wheel, rolling down the windows, blasting some good tunes, and conquering foreign roads. You'll find an agency in any major airport—Avis, Budget, Europcar, Hertz, and Thrifty are all international companies. Some have apps to save you long-ass lines at the airport and frustrating miscommunication. For shorter term rentals, check out Zipcar (which starts at $7 per hour) and Car2Go—which you can pick up/drop off anywhere and use for ten to twenty minute grocery runs.

Not every country requires an Inter-national Driving Permit, but some do. You can get one at your local DMV before leaving. Keep in mind that road signs will be in the language of the country and you'll have to figure out which side of the road to drive on. Be prepared to be confused while in motion.

OTP Tip: Services like Uber and Lyft are great luxuries for when you're lazy, drunk, or far from public transit.

AIRBNB

In recent years, the idea of apartment sharing went from being completely absurd to one of the most popular ways to stay. People all over the world have a little extra space that they can spare and taking advantage of their couch, room, or trailer is your ticket to living on the cheap. Rentals listed on Airbnb are well organized, span the globe, and are reviewed by previous guests to give you an idea of what you're getting yourself into.

AIRBNB PROS

Range
Since people on Airbnb are renting whatever available space they have, you can land yourself on not just a couch but in a backyard tent, airstream, or tree house. People have quirky little hideout spaces in their houses like lofts and guesthouses, so if you're the type that likes to sleep in strange cocoons, this is a great perk.

Group Travel
If you're traveling with more people, locking down an entire apartment is probably easier (and cheaper) than finding a hostel that can accommodate your rowdy bunch. If it's just you and your boo, the privacy element of having an entire apartment or room is a nice break from hostel life.

Hosts
It takes a certain kind of person to welcome a stranger into their home. Usually, hosts are open-minded and excited to meet somebody new. They'll share stories, kitchens, and brewskies and will have insider knowledge on where to eat, drink, and party in their city.

AIRBNB CONS

Hosts
Sometimes the kind of people that welcome strangers into their homes are not quite all right upstairs. You can get a range of weirdos that'll stare at you while you sleep or talk your ear off about crazy-ass shit. Being diligent with reading the host's reviews and comments can weed out some of the weirdos but not all.

Location
Sometimes hosts boast about the surrounding neighborhood of their place in their profile but upon arrival, you realize it's way more out in the sticks than you thought. Carefully reading reviews is key here. If people who previously stayed at the place say nothing about leaving their room, or mention having a car while there, keep those things in mind when booking.

Atmosphere
Airbnb rentals can be a pretty good time if the host is down or not around. Sometimes, though, hosts just need the extra cash and have strict guest and noise policies. Also, if renting in a city, chances are even if your hosts aren't around during your stay, they'll have neighbors they don't want to piss off. Late night ragers are usually out of the question at Airbnbs for these reasons.

OTP Tip: Booking.com is a great resource that searches across hostel, Airbnb, hotels, and other available accommodations, complete with accurate reviews. The upside is you can lock down a place to crash in advance without putting down a cent until the day before you arrive.

COUCHSURFING

With over five million members worldwide, CouchSurfing is a free-to-use network that connects travelers with locals and allows travel enthusiasts to safely flop around on each other's international couches. Sign up as a host, a surfer, or both. If you play the game well, you can get a free place to sleep with the added benefit of a local's perspective on your destination—something you can't always find in a hostel. A general "pay it forward" undertone exists with the hope that you'll host CouchSurfers in your city when you eventually move out of your parents' basement.

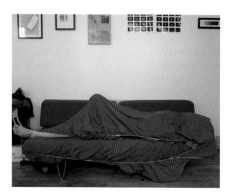

COUCHSURFING PROS

It's Free

Not "free, but gratuity accepted" free, or "free, but you can repay me tonight ... wink, wink" free, but actually free. Monetary payment is strictly prohibited in the Couch-Surfing community, but it's common to find creative ways to give something back.

Hosts

The generous CouchSurfing hosts are normally locals or at least residents who know the area. Usually, they'll have great insider recommendations and may invite you to hang out with some of their local friends. Be grateful. These wallet saviors make CouchSurfing possible.

Community

CouchSurfers in most cities coordinate budget gatherings or events for local and traveling CS-ers, and many hosts accommodate several surfers at once. Also, CouchSurfers are often the brokest of the broke travelers. So if your dinner budget calls for eating crackers in the park, you may find company. The profile count is several million strong and growing. CouchSurfers exist in every country on the planet, and they're normally down to at least meet up and talk shop.

Safety

You are in someone's home, so your stuff should be as safe as everything they own. As for the dilemma of sleeping at a stranger's home, the self-policing of CouchSurfing's active community keeps it very safe—just remember to use common sense. If some dude has a new profile, no friends or recommendations, a picture that resembles Hannibal Lecter, and asks that all CouchSurfing requests include a picture of your feet, you might want to pass. But if your potential host has plenty of recommendations (especially from others in your demographic), an interesting profile, and has been an active member of the community for a while, you should have nothing to worry about.

COUCHSURFING CONS

Not the Backpacker Party Crowd

CouchSurfers are a solid, entertaining group that occasionally party with the best of 'em, but the day-in and day-out hookups and guaranteed debauchery of a party hostel isn't part of the community (which can be a "pro" when your liver needs a rest). Sometimes you may be on your own with a busy, working host, so you'll have to entertain yourself. And, unlike hostel back-packers, CS-ers come in all ages and walks of life.

Range of Comfort

You may get lucky finding someone with a spare bedroom, but usually you're sleeping on a floor mat or (surprise!) a couch in the living room. The host's profile will list the sleeping arrangements, so you'll know what to expect.

Booking

This takes some prep time. You'll first need to set up a profile, post pictures and information about yourself, and get refer-ences from past travel buddies. When your profile is ready, search for hosts in your destination preferably a week in advance (more in high season). Review the pro-files to make sure the location, couch, and host are all to your liking. Download the CouchSurfing app to stay on top of the dialogue.

MORE OPTIONS

CAMPING

For the ultimate freedom while backpack-ing, pitch a tent. Camping connects you to international wilderness and can save you big bucks. Just check the local ordinances and stay away from the tweekers. In Scan-dinavia, there is actually a "right to access" law that allows you to camp on any land, public or private, as long as it's not being farmed and you don't get in people's way. If you buy your gear locally, you'll save your back from lugging it across the world and possibly on baggage fees. The equipment isn't cheap, but it will quickly pay for itself in saved accommodations costs. You can also sell it online once you're all camped-out.

HOTELS

While hotels generally aren't the ideal option, occasionally they make sense. On some islands in Thailand, it costs $2 for a hostel bed or $10 for a private room in a resort with a pool. After months of travel, it's nice to treat yourself and sprawl out naked on a double bed for a few nights (especially if you've found a travel fling). Just remember to return to the backpacker grime before your hands get too soft.

BACKPACKS AND PACKING

Once you're out and about, you'll be surprised at how little you actually need. The less you bring, the more resourceful you'll learn to be.

CHOOSING YOUR BACKPACK

Your pack will be on your back like a nagging spouse whom you can't divorce any time soon. Do not buy a pack online without first giving it an in-person test run. Price is important when picking your pack, but so are your frame size, shape, and determining just how many of those buckles and zippers you need. Employees with experience under their hip straps can suit you up properly. You're looking for something that distributes weight evenly, so don't be afraid to throw some weights in the pack and walk around the store to test it. This is when you ask a lot of questions without worrying about looking or sounding stupid. Once you've found the chosen one, compare prices online and see if you can get a better deal at a different store or online.

OTP BACKPACK TIPS

• Bigger isn't always better. A fifty- to sixty-five-liter pack (about twenty to thirty pounds when stuffed) should do the trick.

• The weight of your world will be on your shoulders and hips–make sure both shoulder and hip straps are padded. Hip straps can take 40 percent of the weight off your shoulders.

• Everybody loves easy access. A zip-front opening is crucial so that getting to your clean underwear isn't a twenty-minute mission.

• Daypacks are super useful. There will be plenty of days when you'll leave your pack at the hostel and want a small backpack for exploration. Some packs come with a daypack built in, but if yours doesn't, choose a regular old backpack that you can wear on your front with your bigger pack on your back.

• Keep all that important shit–passport, money, medicines, phone–in your daypack and guard it like a pit bull.

• Looks really don't matter. You're going to abuse the snot out of this thing. It'll be sat on, used as a pillow, crammed in dirty storage spaces and under buses, and hell, with all those straps, you can even use it as a drying rack for your wet clothes. Stitch on some patches if you're looking for style.

PACKING

This ain't no weekend trip: procrastination packing will leave you in the middle of a shit-storm without a raincoat. Think about the climate you'll be hitting, the weather patterns in the regions you visit, and the duration of your trip. To maximize space, use the roll method. Military-style packing conserves a surprising amount of space and saves you from the dorky crease lines made by folding clothes suitcase-style. Some travelers opt for space-saving bags, which compress clothes and other items in airtight compartments. Medium-size, waterproof stuff sacks are great for organizing too, and can come in handy whenever things get moist.

CLOTHING

No matter which small, dusty, undeveloped corner of the world you're going to, you don't need as much shit as you think. True fashionistas can pull off looking fly with minimal clothes, and you'll want some room in your pack for on-the-road finds. Pack with sacrifice in mind—if you're not sure that you'll need it, you probably don't. You should bring enough clothes to last about two weeks without having to do laundry. A little dirt is part of the backpacker ethos, but leave the whites at home to be more discrete when filthy.

Don't max out your credit card for "traveler wear"—you'd feel like a nerd in zip-off lightweight khakis anyway. Pack two or three pairs of pants you feel comfortable in, both on the dance floor and on the trail. Ladies can replace one pair of pants with an ankle-length skirt for variety. Ankle-length is ideal because you won't trip on it while hauling ass, no one will mistake you for a streetwalker, and it can oftentimes double as a tube dress or long top.

Three or four T-shirts will do the trick. When you're ready for a change, bust out the scissors and turn your T-shirts into tank tops. Two or three good pairs of sweat-resistant, made-for-walkin' socks (wool is the best) will suffice, and three to five pairs of underwear will be fine if you wash them regularly.

Don't take more than three pairs of shoes. You'll want either running shoes or hiking boots, shoes for wandering around or going out, and a pair of flip-flops. Many hostels have shared showers where foot grossities are waiting to take your little piggies to nastyland, and having the flip-flops will save you from fungus.

No matter what weather you're headed into, the importance of a good, lightweight raincoat can't be overstated. Marmot makes a super snazzy one that folds up into its own pocket. Aside from obvious uses, when you couple this puppy with a fleece or a hoodie, you've got your northernmost face covered. Layering is key.

If you're planning on being in wintery climes or high altitudes, pack a good wool hat and scarf, waterproof gloves, and long underwear. Columbia makes some new-fangled long johns that are both sweat-resistant and heat-trapping, and for high-altitude trekking, the investment is worthwhile. Remember, though, you can always stock up on shit when you need it. If you're going somewhere where the dollar is still strong, buying stuff like hats and scarves when you arrive beats lugging them around.

SLEEP GEAR

You'll spend about a third of your trip sleeping, so packing stuff to make downtime comfortable is important. Overnight buses and trains don't come with pillows, and at particularly grungy hostels, it's nicer to sleep on your own drool stains than somebody else's. You'll want a small pillow, preferably an inflatable one that folds up. A sleeping sack can be made for free by sewing up two sides of an old folded sheet—a great, lightweight addition to your pack that allows you to avoid contact with others' bodily fluids. A pack of lightweight earplugs is worthwhile if you're not so into night noises.

If you're planning to sleep with Mother Nature, packing a lightweight sleeping bag can save you from the elements. Tents are a luxury because you'll have to lug around your temporary housing everywhere you go. This gear is often available for rent and your back will thank you later.

BATHROOM ESSENTIALS

Not overpacking toiletries is the easiest way to save on space and weight. Plan on buying extra shampoo and deodorant on the road, even if you can't find your favorite brand. A travel towel made from lightweight, quick-drying material is a must. Sunscreen and bug spray are good to grab before you go; the cost of sunscreen can burn if locals don't use it. Ladies: bring at least a couple weeks' worth of Aunt Flo's favorites in case you can't find them when you need them. And no one should be without at least a few condoms, even if you're not planning on getting busy—you never know. And don't forget your toothbrush.

FIRST AID

You may not be an EMT, but it's worth packing a few essentials like Band-Aids, antibacterial cream, and Steri-Strips (for instantly binding bad cuts) to play it safe. Pharmacies abroad are different than they are at home. While you can sometimes get just about any drug you want—including Valium and Oxy—it can be difficult to find the simple stuff like aspirin or allergy pills. Make sure all of your necessary prescriptions are clearly labeled (so that they're not questioned or taken at security) and you have enough for the duration of your trip. Pack a small bottle of headache medicine (for those nasty hangovers) and something to handle a bad cold. Tap water is a no-no in almost all developing countries. If you're planning on roughing it, bring at least a few water purification tablets—drinking funky water will definitely slow you down and spoil your trip.

SAFETY GEAR

You will need a lock to safely leave your backpack in the hostel locker. An old-fashioned Master Lock will work for some places, but since locker hole sizes vary widely, a lock with a thinner loop is a better bet. If you're super into safety, you might be interested in Pacsafe's stainless-steel locking net device to cover your pack. Packing a money belt depends on how paranoid/much of a nerd you are.

TECH GEAR

Even if you're not the writer type, chances are you'll want a journal and a couple pens to jot down notes, directions, and hotties' digits. Aside from taking decent photos, your phone is crucial for its function as an alarm. This becomes necessary when train and bus schedules require exact wake-up times. Don't forget your charger or a phone case that extends your battery life, a good set of earbuds, and mini speakers for impromptu dance parties. Keep pricey gadgets to a minimum. If you can't easily replace it, don't bother bringing it. Everything else will be available on the road. If not, you will figure out how to either make do without it or whine until someone forks over whatever it is you forgot.

HEALTH
AND SAFETY

Globe-trotting is safer than you think, and arming yourself with awareness is your best defense against bugs and thugs abroad. You can't protect yourself from every incident, but you can take precautions that will help keep your trip worry-free. Using common sense, washing your hands, and being aware of your surroundings goes along way. Here are more specific things we have learned on the road.

HEALTH

IMMUNIZATIONS, DISEASE, AND PARASITES

Generally, places that are least developed are most prone to disease; tropical areas have some nasty bugs (like worms that swim into your pisser), and the world water supply isn't always microbe-free. As a liability catchall, certain areas in the world have been flagged by the United States as "no-go" health zones to deter Americans from traveling there, but that doesn't mean they're actually impossible (or super dangerous) to explore. As long as you have the proper gear and knowledge, there's no need to let the fear-mongers stop you from going anywhere in the world.

SHOOT UP BEFORE YOU HEAD OUT

Depending on where you're headed, you might need to be inoculated against parasites or diseases, particularly in developing countries. To find out which vaccinations are required to visit any country, go to the Cdc.gov, the Centers for Disease Control website. If you want a second opinion, check out the British Foreign and Commonwealth Office (Fco .gov.uk) for their vaccination suggestions, as well.

WATER IS IMPORTANT, BUT BEWARE

Water with microscopic nasties can turn your globe-trotting into a long visit with the crapper. Unless you like impromptu colonics, we suggest you stick to bottled water and avoid ice cubes in drinks when in developing countries. Just drinking booze the entire time will help you avoid the bugs, but might not be so great for staying hydrated (or avoiding cirrhosis). The water in most places in Europe is generally safe, but no matter where you go, read up on what the water situation is for that country.

HEALTH CARE VARIES

You might be pleasantly surprised at the quality of health care available in many places and horrified at others. Some medicines that require prescriptions in the United States are over-the-counter abroad and vice versa. (For instance, topical steroids such as cortisone often need a prescription in other countries, but you can stock up on Viagra without a doctor's note.) There are some areas where meds are hard to come by, so be prepared with common travel antibiotics and a decent first-aid kit. Having some rubbers with you never hurts.

READ UP ON WHAT THE LOCALS KNOW

Following Twitter feeds, reading blogs, and checking out expat forums are all good ways to find out critical information on staying disease-free during your travels. Finding out the scoop from people who live in these areas will give you a heads-up on what's safe and what isn't. For example, when traveling around the sub-Saharan tropics (and some parts of tropical Central and South America), ironing all of your clothes (including your dainties) will kill eggs from the Putzi (or Tumbu) fly, which burrows into your skin.

TRAVEL CLINICS

Travel clinics are the Zen masters of getting you inoculated against the world of internal creepy-crawlies. These are places where doctors specifically see patients who will be traveling, particularly to developing countries, and are a great resource for both getting in good health before your trip and stocking up on info to keep you healthy while abroad. Find your local travel clinic and chat with the doctor about eight weeks before your trip, as some immunizations and meds need time to kick in. If you have insurance, check to see what's covered.

The medical staff will have a lot of questions to ask you about your travels, so try to get at least some of your plans straightened out before you give them a visit. Focus on figuring out which countries you will hit and for how long (the length of your stay sometimes dictates your level of risk and changes the vaccines you may need). Read up on the immunizations suggested for your specific country on the CDC website, and make sure you let the doc know about any current ailments. Once all of your preventative measures are in order, talk to your doctor about getting antibiotics for the road. Fill all your current prescriptions with extras to cover the time you're traveling (remember the liquid carry-on limitations for things like liquid meds and saline solution). You may need to start some regimens (e.g., malaria pills) a few days before you depart. Keep copies of your immunization records with you during your trip.

FIRST AID AND MEDICATIONS

While most countries have well-stocked local pharmacies, it can be a pain trying to find what you want or need, particularly when there is a language barrier and especially if you're not feeling your best. Here are a few of the essentials to take with you for quick fixes on the go.

OVER-THE-COUNTER ESSENTIALS

You can MacGyver yourself into relatively good health using the list of items below. For the heavier stuff, always bring your original prescription in case there's a dispute at the border—but things like diabetic insulin, birth control, allergy, and asthma inhalers should be fine.

- ✈ Antibacterial hand sanitizer
- ✈ Ibuprofen, acetaminophen, and/or naproxen
- ✈ Sunscreen
- ✈ Lip balm
- ✈ Bug spray
- ✈ Band-Aids/blister plasters like Compeed
- ✈ Neosporin
- ✈ Imodium A-D/ Pepto Bismol
- ✈ Preparation H
- ✈ Sleeping/anxiety pills
- ✈ Condoms
- ✈ Thermometer
- ✈ Antinausea/motion-sickness pills
- ✈ Aloe or lidocaine

FOOD

As with water, food around the world contains different things that can shoot through you faster than a hot knife through butter. It's not a pretty thought, but it's worse to be unprepared when you feel the familiar (and painful) gut gurgling begin. Besides the obvious, prolonged diarrhea can cause dehydration, malnutrition, and major discomfort. Treat yourself to authentic food joints, but remember that your body needs time to acclimate to all of the new foods you're shoveling in. If you pile on days of eating unfamiliar foods, your body will rebel against you.

MOSQUITOES

Sharks and Chuck Norris ain't got shit on mosquitoes, the deadliest creature in the world and responsible for over one million deaths annually. In the States, these guys are just biters, but overseas they can be lethal, or, at the very least, make your life miserable for days—if not longer. Mosquitoes can carry malaria, the Zika virus, dengue fever, encephalitis, and yellow fever, among other grizzly shit. If you're going to a tropical area with known mosquito issues, you'll need clothing that will cover you from head to toe and some serious repellant. If you're really hoofing it into the jungle, bring mosquito netting to sleep safely. And talk to the doctor about antimalarials—people from all over the world die every day from malaria transmitted by mosquitoes. They might be tiny, but they're serious.

TRAVEL INSURANCE

If shit hits the fan, having travel insurance is a good backup plan. It's basically protection for when "what if" turns into reality. The issue with insurance is that we never know if—or when—those risks will materialize, and it's pretty likely you'll buy insurance and never use it, which can feel like you've wasted some hard-earned dough. So what do you do?

Well, here's the deal: you know that traveling poses higher risks in all regards, health and safety being two risks that dominate the pool. Buying insurance can help ease your mind. For example, if you need to be immediately evacuated back home for treatment, you will be covered. Oftentimes, insurance will cover theft of almost anything and even the annoying accidents that happen along the way, like dropping your phone into the Seine while trying to get a photo. Think about your worst-case scenario and how much that would cost . . . and then decide if you want to get insurance. Check out WorldNomads.com and TravelGuard.com for some quotes and see what is covered. If you're worried about theft, accidents, or other trip interruptions, make sure those are included in your policy.

KEEPING YOUR JUNK SPOTLESS

When you're living the backpacking dream, your daily itinerary can include things like cliff jumping, dive-bar crawling, and hostel fornicating. The last thing on your mind is genital hygiene. But there comes a time when your junk could really use some personal attention, and there's more to protecting your goods than not touching your wiener with curry-hands. While none of us are doctors, we all definitely have genitalia, and here is what we know about keeping your tools tidy while traveling.

KEEP IT CLEAN

The backpacking community is notorious for random hookups. With so many players in the game, it's important to make sure your equipment is clean and odor-free. Keep the home runs coming with regular showers. Just don't wash yourself raw—scrubbing too hard can cause infection. While your inner-hippie might be tempted to let your pubes grow wild, bear in mind that longer hair means more bacterial growth, which leads to funkier smells. In less-developed countries, getting a wax can be insanely cheap. Take advantage of it and go for that lightning bolt landing strip you've always wanted.

Ladies: the tighter your panties (or pants), the higher your risk of getting a yeast infection. Stick to cotton underwear, or if you're feeling ballsy, go commando. Bidets are a norm in lots of countries, so use these magic inventions to give your kitty an extragood cleaning (or to make her purr if the water pressure's good). Stay away from douches though—like overscrubbing, these can also cause infection.

OTP Tip: Baby wipes are superhandy for cleaning up more than babies.

PLAY IT SAFE

Backpackers are an adventurous bunch—especially in the sack—but don't get carried away and ride bareback. No matter how good your traveler's insurance is, the only coverage for avoiding an STD is to always wrap it up. It takes two to screw—girls should carry condoms, as well. Keep in mind that the risks are different across the world and that not all STDs are visible. Before getting on the plane at all, get tested. Not only is it good karma, but you can also get properly treated for any infections at home instead of at some shady clinic in rural South America.

WHERE TO GET THE GOODS

It's not a bad idea to pick up a big box of condoms at home—it'll be a hell of a lot lighter than the consequences of going without. If you opt to buy them abroad, pick a brand you've heard of and check the expiration date. You'll be able to find them in just about any drugstore, or if you're on a really tight budget, ask around for clinics or hostels that give them away for free. In some countries, it's frowned upon (or even illegal) for a lady to buy a condom, so look up condom laws before you go. In some cities in the Philippines, for example, no one can buy a condom without a prescription.

UTIS (URINARY TRACT INFECTIONS)

These are much more common in women than men. On the road, people tend to get dehydrated from frequent movement and avoidance of contaminated water. Combine this with grimier conditions, and you got yourself a Grade A UTI. Point is: drink lots of water. If you can't find bottled water, use water treatment tablets, which kill most of the evil bastards that will give you the shits and nervous giggles. Pee as often as possible, even if it means popping a squat in a nearby bush. Holding it keeps bacteria trapped in your system and can lead to UTIs. If you're prone, get your doctor to prescribe a course of antibiotics before you go, just in case.

BIRTH CONTROL

If you're a pill-popper, get your prescription filled before leaving and make sure it's enough for the whole trip. Keep an alarm set to the time back home so you know exactly when to take it upon arrival—it can get confusing with time-zone changes and long-ass flights. Taking the pill can be a pain when you're on the road, so consider switching to another form of birth control such as the NuvaRing, Depo-Provera, or the patch. Traveler's antibiotics (like the antimalarial doxycycline) can make the pill less effective, another reason bring rubber backup.

IN CASE OF AN ACCIDENT

Shit happens. Oral contraceptives can fail, and condoms can slip or break, turning a sloppy one-night stand in Barcelona into a Knocked Up-style fiasco. Luckily, the morning-after pill (emergency contraception or EC) is now available in over 140 countries. Check out what EC is available by country before you go, including what's sold over the counter. Remember that EC is only effective for 120 hours (five days) after an accident, and the longer you wait, the less powerful it is. If you're too late for the morning-after pill and can't handle a kid yet, look up the nearest family planning clinic and see what your options are for an abortion. Since abortion is illegal in many places, you may have to travel to another country or return home early.

SAFETY

Every country has different levels of general safety (i.e., likelihood of you getting robbed or hurt). While major crimes do happen, it's unlikely you'll be held up at gunpoint. As fun as a good pistol-whipping might sound, backpackers are normally seen as targets for petty theft and small-time crime. The things working against you:

+ Your huge, necessary-but-obvious backpack.
+ Petty criminals are well aware of the fact that backpackers will have more cash on them than most locals. One stereotype (among many others) about Americans abroad is that they're rich.
+ You will look (and will sometimes be) lost, especially if you're unfolding and looking at a giant map.
+ You don't speak the language.
+ You sleep in train stations (or on trains), on buses, or on beaches to save money—or because you're damn tired from recent travels.
+ Being drunk or high. When you're impaired, the chance that you'll lose your belongings is greatly increased. Criminals know this.
+ You see great things, and you take pictures of those things. People see your phone out, and people want your phone.
+ You're conspicuously messing around on your phone in public—which is like saying, "Here, take my phone. I'm obviously too stupid to have one."
+ Hostels attract a wide variety of characters. Most are awesome, while others would love to relieve you of your possessions.

Here's the reality—as safe as you might feel, you have to be aware that you're always a target. This doesn't mean you should be a twitchy, paranoid mess, but be conscious of your surroundings and take precautions with your valuables.

PROTECT YOUR SHIT

Copy/Photograph Documents

People steal passports because they are worth a lot of money on the black market. So, make three copies of everything (legal ID, passport, birth certificate). Keep one copy on you, one in your backpack, and leave one with a trusted friend or family member. Take a picture of all your documents and e-mail them to yourself. That way, even if you are robbed and stripped naked, you can still easily access and print out your documents. Another easy precautionary measure is to e-mail yourself necessary telephone numbers of your credit card companies (in case cards are stolen), hostels/airlines you've made reservations with, your bank, doctor, and family/friends.

Protect the Backpack

With your backpack on your back, it's pretty easy for thieves to unzip, grab, and run. If you're napping somewhere where you might be vulnerable, use your pack as a pillow, and wrap the extra straps around your wrists. That way, if someone tugs, you'll feel it. If you're walking somewhere you feel particularly unsafe, wear your pack on your front to keep a closer eye on it. It will look like you're in your third trimester, but it's better than having to replace something important.

Travel Locks

Buy a lock to secure your important items in hostels. Hostels usually provide you with lockers, but not locks. It's nice to know your stuff is safe when you're out getting cultured. Travel Sentry (Travelsentry.org) locks are made specifically with travelers in mind and offer designs for different scenarios. They fit on hostel lockers and your backpack zipper lock, as well. They are also recognized and easily opened by US and UK customs officials at all airports. (If they're going to dig through your bag anyway, you might as well make it a faster process.)

Intuition, Attitude, and Common Sense

Stay alert and street-smart while traveling. You have to be assertive and avoid looking nervous, a trait schemers will exploit. Be aware of your surroundings and do not ask strangers to watch your stuff—take it with you even if it's for a quick bathroom break. Do some research on sketchy city regions to avoid, but don't get yourself to a point where you cut off your interaction with locals or deny yourself the ability to take your plans off course.

Avoid old baby mamas and their babies (or cute little begging kids for that matter).

They often use their cuteness, helplessness, and desperation as a decoy to pick the pockets of tourists. Ignore them, check behind you, and walk away quickly.

M&M (MINIMIZE AND MONETIZE)

Minimize: take as little as possible with you when you go out so you have less to carry and less that can be stolen. When going out, take what you need out of your wallet rather than bringing your whole wallet.

Monetize (i.e., keep your eyes on your money): check often to make sure you don't have anything sticking out of your pockets (which is easier to do with less stuff). Try not to carry anything in your back pockets. Since your backside is mostly a layer of fat (it's true), you don't feel as much there, which makes reaching into your back pocket the easiest way for someone to snatch something.

NECK WALLETS AND MONEY BELTS

Neck wallets and money belts are options if you are extra paranoid about the safety of your documents (they're very nerd-chic; maybe more nerd than chic). These are slim pouches that you wear as a necklace or around your waist under your clothes, that can only fit your passport, some emergency cash, and a condom or two (although if you're wearing this, your chances of getting laid diminish significantly). While these things are decidedly unsexy, they can prevent passport theft, because even the most accomplished thieves find it difficult to reach up or down your shirt or pants without you noticing.

POLITICAL UNREST/CIVIL WAR

Many countries are currently in a civil war, are politically unstable, and/or have regular violent protests. Being caught up in a politically fueled situation you are unfamiliar with can be dangerous. Tourists can be kidnapped, caught in crossfire, or just unable to escape the country. Read up on your destination's political climate and decide if visiting it at the moment would be a good idea. However, don't let previous civil unrest stop you from visiting a place, either. Countries like Burundi and Rwanda experienced civil unrest and genocide less than two decades ago, but are now great places for an off-track adventure. Cross-reference the United States Travel Portal and Australia's Travel Advisory to get a wider picture of travel advisories around the world.

THE POLICE

Unfortunately, a country's police force isn't always there to keep you safe—and some-times, it's just the opposite. Corruption within government agencies is not uncom-mon abroad, and many government officials are openly willing to accept bribes. They also know you want to avoid trouble, so cops can be (and sometimes expect to be) paid off. For most developed countries, the police should be approachable, but it's a good idea, particularly when trav-eling in less developed areas, to ask the locals about the police force—and what alternatives you have if you do encounter an emergency.

CAB DRIVERS

Cab drivers are frequent scammers. Since a cab is often a luxury (or a necessity after a long day of travel), here are a few tips to keep you from getting scammed by cabbies:

✈ Insist on a meter or a set price before you get in the cab. In some countries, meters just aren't used, and if that's the case, negotiate the price before the taxi starts moving. It's also a good idea, if you know you'll be taking a cab to a well-known destination, to ask some locals what that route should cost.

✈ If you're nervous about hailing a random cab, call your hostel/hotel and ask them to call a reputable company and have them meet you at a designated location.

✈ While you're in the cab, be aware of the route you're taking. If you have a smartphone and a data plan, follow the cab on a map app like Google Maps. Otherwise, get a city map and follow along. This will help to ensure your cabbie isn't taking you for a ride to get more cash. Feel free to insist on a certain route in advance or while you're on your way.

✈ If a cabbie asks you if this is your first time in the city, your answer is always "no." Tell him or her that you've been here many times, and stop the conversation. While some drivers might just be chatty, others are trying to determine if they can circle the block a few times knowing you won't notice.

✈ In countries where the risk of kidnapping is greater, following the route on a map will give you your bearings, and if you start to feel something is wrong, you can jump out and take off. Always make sure the door handles work from the inside, as well, and don't put your bag in the trunk; keep it with you in the backseat for a quick exit.

✈ Use dedicated taxi lines. In some places, unlicensed or unregulated taxi drivers will approach you and offer you a ride. Most cities have designated taxi lines where the properly licensed taxi drivers will line up.

✈ Have small-currency bills or coins ready. Some cabbies will try and scam you with incorrect change for large bills.

SEX, DRUGS, AND PARTYING

There are lots of fun ways to find yourself abroad, but this part is the most fun to discuss. Sex, drugs, and partying will make your trip memorably mind-blowing and are vital to your worldly experience. You will be hooking up with a whole slew of internationals, and you will have a damn good time doing it (safely, of course). If some drugs find their way on the menu, we won't judge. Moderation is always key (nobody likes a crackhead). As for partying, there are beach, club, hostel, hot tub, and pool parties for the taking abroad. Here are a few things we have learned along the way that should maximize your fun times.

SEX

The conditions abroad are perfect for getting laid. Everyone is so excited to be out of their element that any inhibitions are left far behind. Hooking up with fellow backpackers is inevitable. They're just as horny and are in the same boat with you mentally (sometimes even close to the same bed). Hooking up with locals is more of a challenge, but everybody loves a good chase, right? A few important factors to get you laid by a local:

✈ Looking your best abroad may be hard. Groom, shower, and primp a bit if you plan to get laid. Go grungy when you're in between places. Balance is key.

✈ Smile and be friendly. Sure, the mysterious character is cool, if you think you can play it—just save that card as the ace up your sleeve.

✈ Converse. Talk about where you're from and how much you love traveling. Even if there's a language barrier, let your charm shine through.

✈ Modify your tactics based on your location. Buying drinks and generally being awesome always helps, but knowing a bit of the local ways and hot spots won't hurt your cause.

✈ Culture matters when it comes to sex. Some places are very lenient on the sexual liberation front. Other places, like the Middle East, have very strict hook-up rules, and premarital sex may be out of the question altogether. To get more in the know, here's a list of some our favorite spots for sneaking in a quickie:

BERLIN, GERMANY
The novel ingredients make this cultural melting pot worth a taste. Warehouse clubs, grungy districts, and hidden bars give Berlin's large BDSM crowds proper grounds to play.

SANTORINI, GREECE
Nude beaches, hot backpackers, and world-famous sunsets will help bring some romance back into your stick-it-where-it-fits sex life.

IBIZA, SPAIN
The mecca of electronic music, Ibiza is where you can get your dance on all night, then settle into your beachside shack for some good lovin' before sunrise.

STOCKHOLM, SWEDEN
The Nordic are naughty. With its beautiful, busty blonde babes and tall, large-handed dudes, Sweden is a great place to explore your bisexuality. We're always down for trying new things.

WARSAW, POLAND
This capital city hosts an annual Eroticon festival. Enough said.

SÃO PAULO, BRAZIL
Big booties shake with pride in the thong's birthplace. Unleash your desires on the beach or bring it back to one of the city's hundreds of luxurious sex motels with rental rates by the hour.

DRUGS

Traveling is going to get you feeling all kinds of good. Amid the partying, exploring, and meeting of all kinds of people, there may come a time when you want to take your experience to an even higher level. We won't pack your bowl, draw your line, or strap your arm (hopefully it doesn't come to that), but we are here to help.

SUBSTANCE SPECIFICS

Marijuana is a celebrated soft drug that varies in regard around the world. Amsterdam was once a liberal land that welcomed and catered to pot-smoking tourists with coffee shops that were legally slangin' dubs left and right. Things are changing a bit, but the people's habits

remain. The United States is loosening its shackles on possessing small amounts, but you still wouldn't want to get caught with a couple grams of sticky. Some countries have completely decriminalized pot, while others will lock you up in a heartbeat. As with everything, be careful and know the local laws. In most countries, even though most drugs are illegal, you can still pick up with the right street smarts.

Option A

Your best bet: ask people you know. Hostel mates, especially, but anybody you've come into friendly contact with will suffice. Just work the question into a smooth conversation to see if they can help you out.

Option B

A bit more risky: ask unfamiliar people. As with your first choice, try to make friendly conversation first. This lowers your chance of getting straight-up robbed, and (with enough conversational knowledge) should help you weed out the out-of-uniform cops. Drugs tend to follow the money. Stick around nightlife—bars and clubs especially—and ask patrons, bartenders, or bouncers. Start off by asking for pot (as its use is generally taken more lightly). If that goes well, feel free to shmooze your way into inquiring about some other stuff.

All kinds of drugs will be available everywhere, and their legality will vary from place to place. Take some precaution in buying or using.

PARTYING

A party is to be had anywhere in the world. Your entire experience abroad is going to blend into one big party, and you can find something that fits your specific moods and needs in every country. Some will be organized annual celebrations, others impromptu park and house parties or in the ever-present clubs, bars—even costume balls (during the day, night, morning, and any time in between). A taste of some big guns awaiting your arrival:

+ Oktoberfest in Germany (page 126) (around September 20 to October 10, annually) is an organized shit-show dedicated to international beer consumption and downright messiness.

+ Carnaval in Brazil (page 128) (February 22 to 28, annually) is known worldwide for flooding the Rio's streets with its elaborate costumes (with built-in naked-ness) and wild celebrations.

+ Australia Day (January 26th) is where the country (well, continent) celebrates the discovery (through European settle-ment) of Australia. It's all about beers, barbecues, and beaches.

+ Botellóns in Spain (page 140) are organized park drinking parties. You bring your booze, everyone else brings their booze, and you share. Most large plazas in Spain will hold one around 10:00 p.m. every weekend.

+ Holi (typically the third week in March) is a multiday Hindu tradition that takes food fighting to a grown-up level. Massive crowds flood the streets and douse each other with colorful flour. India serves it up strongest.

+ Every October, Copenhagen pulls out all the kinks with its fringe sex festival Kinky Copenhagen (page 130).

STREET-SMART CHART

	LEGAL DRINKING AGE	AGE OF CONSENT
UNITED STATES	**21** With the exception of a few states that do not enforce underage consumption.	**16-18** With some exceptions (none of which are worth testing out).
THAILAND	**20**	**15**
NETHERLANDS	**16/18** 16 = wine & beer with less than 15% alcohol content 18 = all liquor	**16**
AUSTRALIA	**18**	**16-18 . . .** In Queensland, the age of consent for anal sex is 18.
COLOMBIA	**18**	**14**
INDIA	**18-25** Varies between states. Consumption of alcohol in some states is prohibited.	**18**
RUSSIA	**NONE** While there is no law setting a legal drinking age, selling alcohol to minors is prohibited.	**16**
AFGHANISTAN	**ILLEGAL** Those who buy, sell, or consume alcohol can be fined, imprisoned, or given 60 lashes with a whip.	**MOOT POINT** All sexual activity outside of marriage is against the law.
NORTH KOREA *UNCITED CLAIM	**18**	**15**

MARIJUANA LAW	PROSTITUTION LAWS	AVG. PRICE FOR 20 CIGARETTES (USD)	AVG. PRICE FOR A PINT OF BEER (USD)
PARTIALLY LEGAL Decriminalized, medical, and nonmedical usage is allowed in more than 30 states.	**ILLEGAL IN ALL BUT ONE STATE . . .** Nevada (Viva Las Vegas, baby!)	**$6.00** $11.00+ in NYC	**$2.49**
EXTREMELY ILLEGAL Death penalty is possible for drug offenses under Thai law.	**ILLEGAL, BUT . . .** Tolerated & partly regulated. Prostitution is practiced openly throughout the country.	**$2.15**	**$2.07**
LEGAL . . . Considered a "soft" drug, it's sold at coffee shops "under certain strict conditions."	**LEGAL AND REGULATED**	**$8.00**	**$2.77**
PARTIALLY LEGAL Decriminalized and medical allowed.	**ILLEGAL** Brothels and soliciting sex are not allowed.	**$18.00**	**$6.00**
PARTIALLY LEGAL Decriminalized and medical allowed.	**LEGAL . . .** As long as it is done in designated "tolerance zones."	**$2.00**	**$1.20**
PARTIALLY LEGAL Used during observance of certain Hindu rituals. Government-owned shops in holy cities sell cannabis in the form of "bhang."	**LEGAL** Though soliciting in a public place, keeping a brothel, pimping, and pandering are outlawed.	**$3.00** Though Western brands cost much more than traditional hand-rolled "Bidis."	**$1.50**
ILLEGAL, BUT . . . Possession of up to 6 grams is decriminalized.	**ILLEGAL, BUT . . .** Not considered a serious crime. However, organizing prostiution is punishable by imprisonment.	**$1.12** "Budget" brands cost $0.50 on average.	**$2.00**
ILLEGAL Though a popular cash crop for farmers and heavily trafficked on the black market.	**ILLEGAL** With punishments ranging from 5 to 15 years of imprisonment.	**$3.00**	**ILLEGAL**
*LEGAL Statements claim North Korea either has no law against the sale and consumption of weed or it is decriminalized.	**ILLEGAL** According to the North Korean government, prostitution does not exist, but is practiced discretely.	**N/A** *According to 2008 North Korean media reports, 54.7% of the population smokes.	**$2.00**

PART 3

MAKE YOURSELF USEFUL

Backpacking is a learning experience all on its own. You'll interact with a multitude of cultures on an intimate level, digging deep to see how people really live. When you decide it's time to add even more value to your vagabonding (or if you just want to give yourself a reason to stay longer), consider working, studying, or volunteering abroad. The best approach to applying yourself while traveling is to first pin down what you're most interested in. If you're all about educating kids, keeping our planet green, cuddling endangered species, helping to alleviate the impact of disease, or fighting for human rights, we've got something for you to get passionately involved in.

ANIMALS

Animals around the world suffer, mainly because of humans, and there are many ways to use your petting hand for something more meaningful. Supersize your love for felines in South America, test out your veterinary skills in Honduras, and do it like Darwin in the Galápagos. Pick your favorite four-legger (two or none-leggers also work), pack a squeaky toy, and get yourself in a furry situation.

BEST PLACES TO BIRD-WATCH FOR CREDITS

The world has much to offer if you're a bird nerd or just into checking out wildlife beyond the squirrels at your local park. Studying ecology abroad exposes you to indigenous species you may not find at home and places you in the cultural thick of it, allowing you to scope out ecosystems while you get to know the people who inhabit them, all while racking up credits.

ECUADOR'S BLUE BOOBIES

Ecuador is home to the blue-footed booby, a bird with superblue feet. Thanks to a partnership between Boston University and Universidad San Francisco de Quito in Ecuador, you can get credits toward your ecology degree while studying some of the world's most coveted endemic species. This intensive, semester-long program offers students a chance to get their hands filthy in three completely different ecosystems—montane forest, tropical rain forest, and coastal habitats—while simultaneously learning Spanish. Not only do you get to study for four weeks in the Amazon, but also they hook you up with an eight-day trip to the Galápagos Islands, the animal inhabitants of which inspired a little theory you may have heard about. There, you can hack it like Darwin and witness the mating rituals of the waved albatross while making friends with all kinds of tortoises and iguanas.

BATSHIT-CRABBY IN NORTH AFRICA

The archipelago hangs out in the Indian Ocean on the eastern coast of North Africa and is made up of Pemba Island and Zanzibar, along with a bunch of tiny little islets. While the islands are not as biodiverse as mainland Africa, the shrews, monkeys, mongooses, and colorful lizards here will still blow your mind. To give your animal escapades some structure, sign up for the SIT (School for International Training) Study Abroad program (Sit.edu). During the fifteen-week course, you get to shoot the shit in Swahili during one of two home stays on Pemba—where you can observe the rare, endemic Pemba fruit bats in action. Plan on setting aside some quality time with the red colobus monkeys during an excursion to the Jozani Forest, and then go snorkel-crazy on the underwater wildlife off the islets of Bawe, Changuu, Misali, Mbudya, and Sinda. Once you resurface, don't think you're trippin' balls when the boulders grow claws. The coconut crab is the largest arthropod in the world and crawls around these shores making other crabs look like bird food (it also eats meat sometimes).

WHALES AND TAILS IN AUSTRALIA

If you have always dreamed of being the Little Mermaid (or Little Merman), this is your opportunity to explore a whole new world under the sea. The Education Abroad Network (EducationAbroadNetwork.org) offers semester-abroad programs in Sydney with some major perks. Before school even starts, you can poke around the Great Barrier Reef and do some white-water rafting and bungee jumping during their presemester summer program. When it's time to (sort of) hit the books, the 12-week program takes care of 12 credits applicable to your general education with courses in film, literature, photography, economics, music and environment, with employment assistance to earn some extra cash while you work on your degree and your tan.

BIG CATS OF THE AMAZON

The South American jungles conjure up images of jaguars lurking in trees and cougars feasting on deer carcasses. But if you take a trip to the Amazon jungle or Pantanal, you'll have a tough time spotting them. They're not just being big pussies—these animals have been hunted to near extinction in the past century. Conservation efforts have stabilized their numbers, but deforestation, the overhunting by humans of their natural prey, and killing by local farmers to protect livestock keep their future uncertain. Black market dealings also still happen—big cats are hunted for their fur, and moms are killed and babies kidnapped to sell as exotic pets. Here's how to properly get your paws dirty to help these felines.

COMUNIDAD INTI WARA YASSI (CIWY), BOLIVIA

In the 1980s, a couple of Bolivian kids saw firsthand the devastation from unregulated deforestation. At the same time, they witnessed widespread animal abuse—from malnourished circus cats to monkeys forced to get drunk and dance for locals. What started as a pinky swear between friends to protect animals and the environment has turned into an internationally acclaimed environmental conservation effort and an animal rescue and rehabilitation center. Today, CIWY has three sanctuaries where volunteers can work directly with big cats—feeding, walking, and caring for them. This is the best cougar action you'll find outside of a La Paz *boliche*.

PANTHERA, BRAZIL

The biggest and best big cat conservation effort in the world, Panthera is at the top of their kitty-saving game. Recently, when the government of Mongolia wanted to allow the hunting of some almost-extinct snow leopards for "research," Panthera fought back Genghis-hard and got the proposal overturned. Their South American branch is based in Brazil's Pantanal region, home to the largest concentration of jaguars in the world. Local farmers often shoot jaguars to protect their cattle herds, so Panthera is educating locals, observing jaguar behavior, and developing protected corridors and regions for the cats. They work on a wide scale with wild jaguars, cheetahs, pumas, and other big cats, so volunteer and work opportunities are more along the lines of data collection, grant-writing, and necessary administrative duties than petting and taking pictures with kittens.

OTP Tip: Beware! Volunteers love the big cats, and every animal shelter knows this. Some opportunists actually keep cats around solely to attract volunteers—and volunteer dollars—rather than rehabilitating and rereleasing them. Don't get conned. Check various reviews online (not just the organization's website), or find a listing of trustworthy programs—VolunteerSouthAmerica.net is a great place to start.

VISIT THESE ANIMALS BEFORE THEY'RE FOSSILS

Magellanic Penguin
Named after Magellan, these are the largest penguins in the world. Instead of the tuxedo getup, they sport a horseshoe pattern and shed their eye feathers during the warm months.

Endangered because . . . their fishy food supply is currently being threatened by over-fishing, and they waddle into fishing nets and get covered in oil.

Still kickin' it in . . . Argentina, Chile, Falkland Islands

Colombian Woolly Monkey
Fuzzy and woolen, these monkeys use their incredibly strong tails to swing through the Amazon with ease. What have you done with your fifth limb lately?

Endangered because . . . fewer trees in the Amazon means fewer branches on which to swing in avoidance of predators, like jaguars, eagles, and humans, who snatch them up and sell them illegally as pets.

Still kickin' in . . . Colombia and Venezuela

Schmidt's Lazy Toad
The true embodiment of the toad, these frogs are terribly ugly, with warts dotting their bodies, long, lanky legs, and see-through underbellies. They mostly live on land, shamefully hiding under rocks until mating season, where they pop into the water for a quickie.

Endangered because . . . they're actually pretty lazy (or rather, confined to a small area where they thrive). Since their habitat is so limited, and their numbers small, any change to their environment may wipe them out for good.

Still kickin' it in . . . southern and central China

Blue Bustard
Like an obese tenor, this bird has the voice of a frog and makes little croaking sounds to communicate with other bustards in the bunch.

Endangered because . . . the more we mow down their home turf, the less they can croak around freely.

Still kickin' it in . . . South Africa and Lesotho

Striped Legless Lizard
If a lizard has no legs, isn't it basically a snake? Science tells us that their evolutionary histories–snakes never had legs and legless lizards once did–distinguish them greatly.

Endangered because . . . their habitat is being invaded by two-leggers with tractors, and these lizards don't like to slither on concrete.

Still kickin' it in . . . Australia

VETS OF THE WORLD

So you like little furry animals and want to make sure they're safe and sound worldwide? Well, World Vets International is an organization that'll take your love and transform it into action. It costs $40 to join and will put you in the running for some amazing vet programs worldwide. With programs ranging from spaying and neutering programs to hanging with elephants, in countries like Honduras, Thailand, and Mexico, you can fill your travel itinerary while filling your heart with warm fuzzy creatures. Here are five destinations where caring for Fido will get you far.

ROATÁN, HONDURAS

This program is operated on the gorgeous island of Roatán. You will have hands-on experience making sure that the island's furry residents get the care they need. The vet team will operate a field condition sterilization campaign and provide medical consultations to those in need. A big goal here is to eradicate zoonotic disease—or ailments that can be passed from humans to animals—on the island.

CHIANG MAI, THAILAND

What if we told you that you could surround yourself with 450 dogs, 250 cats, horses, birds, rabbits, and pigs in the middle of an elephant sanctuary? Hit up the Thailand program, and living your Dr. Doolittle dream will be a reality. What's more, this volunteer opportunity costs a big fat nothing (if you've paid your $40 membership fee to the World Vets organization).

GRANADA, NICARAGUA

The program started operating out of Nicaragua in 2008, and has since helped build the Latin America Veterinary Training Center. Here, you'll be assisting with surgical procedures and generally helping people and their beloved companion animals get access to veterinary care in a region where it would otherwise be unavailable.

COZUMEL, MEXICO

That same place where your basic beezy friends go to work on their tan lines and alcohol tolerance for spring break also hosts a great hands-on program for polishing your puppy vet skills. World Vets International started in Cozumel—where its CEO was inspired over ten years ago to bring much-needed veterinary care—and the program here consists of helping to spay and neuter local animals.

OTAVALO, ECUADOR

Established in 2009, the Ecuador program's focus is to eliminate the need for animals to be killed by poisoning as a form of population control. World Vets buddied up with local municipalities to provide spay and neutering services to keep animal populations at bay and in return, the government promised to not eliminate the cute cats and dogs hanging out around town. This program is tough in that the volume of sterilizations performed reaches upward of seventy to eighty per day.

DISEASE

While working to help alleviate AIDS is a well-publicized (and important) issue, hunger, lack of clean water, and various other diseases also affect the health of the world's population on a large scale. Opportunities are available in a wide array of settings, from hospitals to school clinics, healthcare offices to out in the field, digging wells to create clean water supplies. While you don't need to be a doctor to help, if you're studying medicine, getting your bearings by working or volunteering abroad would add a lot of value to your MD résumé.

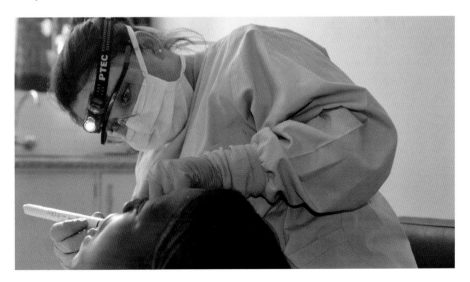

HALF FULL: CLEAN WATER VOLUNTEER PROGRAMS

Our world is royally screwed when it comes to water. One out of every eight people in the world don't have access to sufficient drinking water—that's nearly a billion people. Some women and girls in less developed African countries walk four hours each day to retrieve water, a hike that leaves them wide open to heat strokes and attacks by humans or animals. The time it takes to *just get water* makes it difficult to find time for schooling, and what they do end up retrieving often resembles porta-potty slush—sometimes because it is. One out of every four people in the world (two fucking billion people!) doesn't have a toilet. More people have cell phones than have toilets. This lethal combination of water shortage and contamination affects 840,000 people a year. Half are children. These numbers are no doubt hard to swallow.

While the task of fixing this seems overwhelming, there are many organizations fighting the global water crisis. Wells are dug, boreholes are constructed, pumps are installed, pipes are laid, and new water-purification methods are constantly being tested and implemented. When looking to volunteer with an NGO (nongovernmental organization), be sure they have funding transparency and ask about their sustainability plans. A water pump that breaks after nine months does a community no good if they have no mechanic, parts, or money to fix it. Here are a couple nonprofits to get your search started.

WORLD WATER CORPS

World Water Corps (WWC)—the field division of Water for People (WaterFor People.org)—researches communities and locations in developing nations that have a safe-water crisis. Data is collected and analyzed intensely to ensure a sustainable location is set up within a dedicated community. WWC not only makes it a point to engage the communities, but also relies on them 100 percent to dig the wells themselves and construct the latrines. It becomes a personal investment for everyone in the community, and not just a handout. WWC is on-site to monitor the entire operation, but in reality it becomes a project by the community, for the community. They have projects in developing nations worldwide and take volunteers to help with data collection, monitoring, and analysis of fieldwork. If you're more hands than numbers, start your own fund-raiser with Crowdrise, a WWC partner that helps turn your marathon, mountain climb, or quirky idea into moneymaking machine for the cause.

WATER.ORG

Cofounded by Matt Damon, this organization raises awareness and funds for areas of the world that do not have safe drinking water or sanitation. They organize fund-raisers and solicit donations, emphasizing that every small amount can help—just $25 can give someone water for life. Then they partner with local NGOs to organize and fund a sustainable water solution project that involves the community. The organization appeals to wallets, and we all know yours is empty. Instead, check their website for info about which current and future local NGOs they are sponsoring. Hit up those NGOs and find out how you can get on the ground and get your hands wet.

WATER MISSIONS INTERNATIONAL

This top-rated nonprofit has implemented safe water solutions in over forty-nine countries for more than two million people. While it is a Christian Engineering Ministry, you won't be doing any Bible-thumping. Fieldwork is completely dedicated to engineering and implementing sustainable safe water projects, and they already have an impressive track record of doing so. WMI (WaterMissions.org) is well funded because god-gobblers love giving to charities, and they are on track for being a global safe water-solutions leader. They conduct internships abroad and at their headquarters in Charleston, South Carolina.

RAIN CATCHER

Operating on the principle that "there is no shortage of water given by nature—only a shortage of water being received efficiently by us," RainCatcher (RainCatcher .org) harvests, filters, and distributes rainwater on-site to those who need it. They work on a one-to-one principle: a $1 donation gets one person clean water to drink. Volunteers come in the form of ambassadors—or individuals that start creative campaigns, like Push-ups for Uganda, a fund-raising project started by Tyson Mayr where he would do 10,000 push-ups in ten countries in exchange for funds raised for the program. The organization seeks ambassadors to create fund-raising campaigns that let them turn rainwater into liquid gold.

OTP Tip: Tyson Mayr is the current "Global Water Ambassador" and the sexiest Australian we've ever met. Tyson passionately volunteers to help the organization by bringing awareness to current projects and strongly believes in "travel with a cause." You can be just like him; don't forget leg day.

THE SHOWER DISCREPANCY

Washing off travel funk is a small luxury after a long day of trains, buses, and rickshaws, but Americans are notoriously stereotyped as water wasters. From three-minute power showers to day-long ritual baths, cleanliness customs differ around the world. You might find goofy shower contraptions, bathing in rivers, timed showers to conserve water, or, that the locals forego bathing altogether. Knowing how people deal with dirt will help you look less like a douche.

China: City vs. Country

In rural China, bathing is rare. Due to the lack of access to adequate water, some villagers in western China never bathe, or, at most, will hose down once a month. In the big cities, however, the Chinese bathe like Westerners, and will visit formal bathhouses to relax at the end of a long day. While some are coed, you may be sorted by sex organs upon entering.

Australia: Sing to Save

Australians are encouraged by the government to conserve water due to the lack of natural freshwater resources. Many locals will turn off the shower while soaping-up or time themselves to prevent dawdling. Energy Australia (one of the country's largest power suppliers) encourages its customers who sing in the shower to sing shorter songs–even sending out suggestions of songs that are under two minutes long.

Germany: Letting It All Hang Out

Known not only for its nude beaches, Germany is also splattered with pure thermal watering holes where spa towns have sprung up to soak locals and tourists alike. Most of these coed spas are nude only because bathing suit chemicals are said to taint the water (and we've been worried about urine this whole time!). Baden-Baden is the most famous town with its two main spas, Friedrichsbad (a formal, seventeen-step bathing ritual) and Caracalla (a more relaxed, theme park atmosphere).

Nicaragua: Power Shower

In Nicaragua, showers are often heated at the showerhead (versus in the plumbing behind the wall) by a small electrical converter. If you think it seems like a bad idea to mix electricity and water, it is. These contraptions electrocute several people each year. Best to shower cold and feel refreshed (and stay alive).

WORKING WITH THE RED CROSS

In 1859, thousands of Italian, Austrian, and French soldiers died at the Battle of Solferino, some because they didn't have access to immediate medical care. Moved by the carnage, Swiss businessman Henry Dunant worked to set up national relief organizations, known as Red Cross Societies, for soldiers returning from war. Dunant's movement spread, and, in the 1880s, the red crescent emblem was introduced and used alongside the iconic red cross. Today there are 188 individual Red Cross and Red Crescent National Societies.

These national societies make up one part of the International Red Cross Red Crescent Movement. The movement also encompasses the International Committee of the Red Cross (ICRC), and the International Federation of Red Cross and Red Crescent Societies (IFRC). Combined, these organizations form the largest humanitarian network in the world.

Working or volunteering with Red Cross Red Crescent is as real as it gets. Their main mission is to provide aid through the protection of life and health—and to uphold the dignity of those affected by armed conflict and other disasters. Each branch of the movement has specific objectives, carried out by completely independent teams of employees and volunteers.

NATIONAL SOCIETIES OF THE RED CROSS RED CRESCENT

Millions of Red Cross Red Crescent volunteers work in their home countries across the globe. Among other things, the American Red Cross (ARC) provides assistance for victims of natural disasters like hurricanes, wildfires, and tornadoes. Volunteers work closely with survivors and members of the greater community. This type of volunteering is an essential test run to see if a career in international humanitarian work is up your alley. There are ARC opportunities in communities all across the States.

INTERNATIONAL FEDERATION OF RED CROSS RED CRESCENT SOCIETIES

Founded in 1919, the IFRC acts as a parent organization to Red Cross and Red Crescent National Societies across the world. Job postings change depending on need, but they range from a Reporting Delegate to a Health Coordinator to an IT and Telecommunications Guru. You'll need experience working with humanitarian organizations (like the American Red Cross) if you want to apply. Postings are located everywhere, from Switzerland to Senegal, Bolivia to Bangladesh. The IFRC doesn't assign international volunteer opportunities, or coordinate exchanges between national societies.

INTERNATIONAL COMMITTEE OF THE RED CROSS (ICRC)

More than 12,000 people work in eighty countries under the umbrella of the ICRC. The Committee coordinates field missions meant to alleviate the suffering caused by armed conflict, and deploys workers to emergency zones at the drop of a hat. ICRC staff members are trained professionals who apply for posts around the world as psychologists, surgeons, translators, and agricultural engineers. They work with local law enforcement to maintain international human rights law and visit detainees and prisoners of war. The ICRC also oversees a program to maintain water supplies and sanitation in conflict zones under its Water and Habitat Unit.

While the intention of the Red Cross and Red Crescent movement is always to do good, individual organizations have faced criticism for negligence and lack of forethought. The American Red Cross has faced fire for mixing up samples from blood drives, and individual chapters were caught not using 9/11 fund-raising money for its intended purpose. International Red Cross and Red Crescent organizations have been tainted with similar corruption. On the other hand, because Red Cross and Red Crescent staff consists of highly trained professionals and local volunteers, any one of their organizations offers on-the-ground, hands-on, and rewarding work. Despite corruption allegations and human error, Red Cross and Red Crescent work is committed to a deep-rooted understanding of the community it serves. It's a prestigious gig and can be a perfect fit if you're looking to settle down abroad.

BEST MD YOU CAN BE

Get your premed requisites out of the way while prodding the world and having a damn good time doing it. All the cultural knowledge you'll gather through foreign barhopping, city-touring, and sightseeing will do wonders for your bedside manner later in life. Before you commit most of your twenties to hitting the med school books, check out our list of the best places to be while you're chasing your MD.

LONDON

Pound for pound, London is becoming the strongest sale for studying abroad. Its history, style, entertainment, and entire experience will have your mind radiating with culture shock while the luxury of the same spoken language will keep you feeling comfortable enough to ask the waiter exactly what's in that scary-looking plate (hint: it's pig's cheeks). Specific premed programs are set up in King's College—with focuses on biomedical sciences and clinical experience—and University College London, which hones in on international health policy studies.

COPENHAGEN

The Danish lifestyle is sweet as ever, and studying here is the best way to take a bite out of what the country's got to offer. The Danish Institute for Study Abroad (Disabroad.org) makes your transition to living and studying in Denmark easy, and Copenhagen's easygoing and friendly way of life makes it fun. Plenty of medicine and health-policy programs offered by Denmark International Studies will keep you on your premed path, while the city's utopian transit system and easy intercountry connectivity will keep your more travel-minded path well trod, too.

AUSTRALIA

Shake up your collegiate career by taking your studies Down Under. Not just cool for cuddly koalas and kangaroos, Australia's got plenty of sights to see and places to backpack while fulfilling the educational requirements to keep Mom and Dad (or whoever's floating the bill) satisfied. With one of the largest research institutions in the country, you can study grand-scale subjects like health and society or cultural studies in health at the University of Melbourne. Head to the nation's capital to study medicine with a close-to-home approach and sign up for classes at the University of Sydney, which offers courses in community and indigenous health.

INDIA

The birthplace of *ayurveda* and the frequent source of everything that's weird and interesting about alternative medicine, India is a great place for a med-head. Various programs are available in beachy Kerala, where you can watch locals prepare medicinal plants and smell the healing scents of ancient alternative medicine. For a more

Western approach, check out the medical healthcare internships offered by Gap 360 (Gap360.com), a well-established company offering programs in various areas of study.

WHAT YOU CAN DO FOR AIDS RELIEF RIGHT NOW!

Most prevalent in Africa and Asia, HIV/AIDS disease has affected every population around the world and continues to claim the lives of millions of people annually. While we're no longer in the midst of the '90s wave of awareness campaigns, there is still much work to be done to help those affected.

ADVANCE-AFRICA

Available in Ethiopia, Malawi, Senegal, Uganda, Tanzania, or Kenya, these programs run for a minimum of two weeks. You can choose to work as a teacher at an orphanage or with an HIV/AIDS medical program. Med students and aspiring doctors are in top demand for the medical programs, and volunteers have the opportunity to do either lab research or hands-on medical work. In Kenya, Advance-Africa (Advance-Africa.com) offers travel programs that allow volunteers to assist in the remote villages of the Maasai tribe.

WORLDWIDE HELPERS

This UK-based company (Worldwide Helpers.org) has connected over 37,000 do-gooders with low-cost or no-cost volunteer opportunities around the world. Creating a free account with the organization gives you access to hundreds of great projects. Among them are a variety of HIV/AIDS education and community outreach programs in Africa.

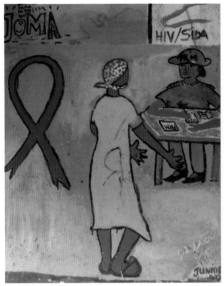
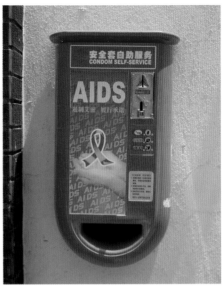

AIDS RELIEF FOR CHINA (ARFC)

If you've got your own ideas about how to combat AIDS, ARFC (Arfcusa.org) is a charity that hooks up people on a mission with the funds necessary to make it possible. In 2004, ARFC worked with the Pen Pal Kids Club to connect rural kids affected by HIV/AIDS with urban volunteers. In 2008, ARFC began facilitating Heart Talk support groups for gay men in more than thirty Chinese cities. You can either contact ARFC about volunteer opportunities with existing programs, or pitch your own charitable idea and apply for an ARFC grant to make it a reality.

GLOBAL VOLUNTEER NETWORK (GVN)

This organization was started in 2000 by a New Zealander who felt volunteer opportunities were far too limited by program fees. While GVN (GlobalVolunterNetwork. org) isn't directly focused on AIDS relief, they do offer many programs in the field and aim to place volunteers directly into communities in need of their specific skills. The Remote Orphan Care Project in rural Uganda is good for camp-counselor types, where volunteers help to organize games, assist with basic schooling, and provide age-appropriate AIDS education. The HIV/AIDS program in Kenya is a crash course in psychology, where volunteers help with homecare visits and counsel community groups. With all kinds of projects in sixteen countries, GVN's network includes some of the most interesting and hands-on volunteer opportunities in the world.

5 COOLEST LIBRARIES AROUND THE WORLD

To safeguard libraries from analog death, modern book houses are spruced up with crazy cool architectural details and new forms of media to keep you people comfortable and entertained while being informed. Don't go moaning and groaning about visiting a library while you're traveling just yet—here are five around the world where books are bottom shelf stuff.

Delft, Netherlands
DOK Library Concept Center

DOK is dubbed the most modern library in the world, but the people who run the place like to think of it as a library concept center—how a library could and should be. You know, with video games, music listening pods, comfy chairs, and not a single shush-er to ruin your brainstorm sesh.

Vancouver, Canada
Central Library of Vancouver

Central Library is the biggest branch off the mindfucking-ly huge Vancouver Public Library tree (which consists of twenty-two total branches). Library Square takes up an entire city block, looks like Rome's Coliseum and houses the seven-story, all-glass Central Library as its centerpiece.

Birmingham, United Kingdom
Library of Birmingham

Europe's largest library is described by its designer as a "people's palace," and its purpose is to make library visits not suck so much. That iridescent exterior will definitely draw you in, and the panoramic cityscape views of Birmingham from inside will free you from library claustrophobia. For some air, head out to one of its several terraces, or even to the rooftop garden. Looking for total entertainment immersion but too lazy to read? There are art galleries, multimedia sections (think music, movies and games), and even a performance stage that holds regular events.

Sendai, Japan
Sendai Mediatheque

The Sendai Mediatheque wanted to stay away from boring-ass library stereotypes, so it slashed the library tag off its title in favor of "mediatheque." This place definitely transcends traditional libraries, and it was made to be entirely transparent to communicate Sendai's clear vision for the future. The first floor has a café and shops, and the seventh (top) floor has a small cinema that screens regular films. In between top and bottom, you'll find art galleries, more multimedia selections, small relaxing rooms, and a vast collection of ancient artifacts (i.e., books) on dusty shelves.

Bishan, Singapore
Bishan Public Library

Libraries are like information ecosystems, so it's only right that the public library in Bishan was designed to look like a tree house. Its glass structure lets in natural sunlight, which filters through colorful windows and creates a pretty trippy ambience, perfect for a break from hectic traveling.

KIDS

As the cliché goes, "children are our future." By jumping into kid-centered work, study, and volunteer programs, you get to participate in the formative years of our world's population. Helping a child learn English (or just a few new soccer moves) may be the spark they need to lead a happy, productive life. Also, hanging out with kids is the best way to get insider intel on any given culture. Win–win.

BITTER CHOCOLATE
CHILD LABOR IN THE IVORY COAST

There's a bitter problem lingering around the production of chocolate. Cocoa farms in the Ivory Coast—which supply major companies like Hershey and produce over a third of the world's cocoa—enslave tens of thousands of kids as young as ten years old to crop their fields. Kids are overworked and beaten regularly, all in the name of turning cocoa beans into green. While the issue has gained some global awareness and caused consumer outrage, the major problem has not yet melted away.

WHAT'S GOING ON

At the turn of the millennium, the dark side of chocolate was confronted, and the Cocoa Protocol came into effect, a program that aimed to eliminate child labor in cocoa production. Years later and leading up to today, children in the Ivory Coast and all along West Africa are still being forced to work 100-hour weeks at low (if any) pay cropping cocoa plantations. Some are ripped from or sold by their families while others voluntarily go, lured by the false promises of food and pay; many even arrive through the sex trade that spans the continent. Upon arrival at their "jobs," all of these children face regular beatings, starvation, and exhaustion while working in the fields.

DO SOMETHING

Mega companies like Hershey and Mars claim that tracing the sources of all of their products is next to impossible, which is why the problem persists. We think that's a shitty excuse, and here's how you can help.

Stop Fueling the Fire

Americans alone spend over $16 billion a year on chocolate, much of which comes from the Ivory Coast. Seek out Fair Trade chocolates instead, which are produced without slave labor—or just lay off the sweets. Some great-tasting, good-feeling companies include Equal Exchange, Madécasse, and Dagoba. The money is the motivator; until your dollar is missed, mega companies like Hershey and Mars won't soon change their methods.

Get Over There

Put up against the standard of living in complete poverty, working in this environment seems like a more productive way of life. Uneducated, hungry, and poor, children in this region often opt for manual labor because no better option is available. Volunteer organizations are set up throughout the continent and are the best means through which you can give these kids something better to live for. Kids Worldwide (KidsWorldwide.org) is a unique organization that is approaching kid-focused development in Africa by cutting out the moneymaking middlemen who normally stand between you and volunteer projects. An organization run by volunteers for volunteers, Kids Worldwide "scaffolds" existing grassroots projects and helps develop them until they become self-sustainable (usually for about five years).

As such, opportunities at Kids Worldwide are multifaceted. You can volunteer to help in project development or jump into an already self-running program in schools and orphanages in many areas of

Africa, like Ghana and Sierra Leone. The children forced into making chocolate to feed our need never get to taste the products of their slave labor. Volunteer to help stop this cruel practice and take a bit of bitterness out of these sweets.

BEST PLACES TO TEACH ENGLISH ABROAD

Homebred Americans, Brits, and Aussies have a skill that's in high demand in many parts of the world: English. Your native language is pretty much The Man when it comes to business, education, and foreign affairs, and the need for English-language teachers is higher than the supply. Some language-based volunteering opportunities focus on teaching kids, while others are all about adults. Either way, the experiences you'll gain being the head honcho of a classroom will look good on your résumé and feel great in the soul.

Before you start packing your bags, make sure you've done your research. Your contract should be transparent in terms of duration, duties, and compensation, and you need to read it closely. You don't want to be blindsided by a situation where you're stuck longer than you want, or get into more than you signed up for. Teaching abroad isn't just about making money or having the ability to wander longer. You're fueling the future by filling in-demand voids.

CHINA

The world's fastest-growing economy wants native English speakers like MSG wants noodles, and the swelling market ensures competitive salaries and great perks. As could be expected, certification regulation isn't terribly stringent—a bachelor's degree is usually enough. Respectful students and community-oriented people will help to temper the cultural shock and send you home with some bones in your pocket at the end of the school year. Check out the English teaching programs at the Council on International Education Exchange (Ciee.org).

SOUTH KOREA

Riding high on the Asian TEFL/ESL boom, teaching English at one of many South Korean gigs offers perks like free accommodations, insurance benefits, and return airfare. Contracts usually last for a year, and the low cost of living outside of ultramodern Seoul affords plenty of time to save up a respectable salary. Be warned: you'll need to brush up on regional cultural norms before you go because Korean social etiquette can be a bit tricky. South Korea also boasts the world's highest-estimated national IQ and the most sophisticated IT infrastructure on the planet. So bring the smarts, hard. You can rest assured it's legit: the Korean government has introduced English program initiatives such as English Program in Korea (EPIK) and Teach and Learn in Korea (TaLK).

CZECH REPUBLIC

Though you'll have to apply for a special work visa if you're not one of those lucky EU passport-holding bastards, teaching in the Czech Republic is your ticket to

history's playground. There's a supertight expat community here, and the beer is literally cheaper than water. If you're looking for a place with plenty of weekend-trip opportunities, you've hit gold—the country is landlocked by Germany, Poland, Slovakia, and Austria. Prague is where the party's at, but if cultural immersion is what you're after, consider teaching in a smaller town such as Plzeň or Brno. The weekly English-language newspaper, *The Prague Post*, is a good source to browse while looking for jobs from home. Check out TEFL Worldwide Prague (TeflWorldwidePrague.com) for additional information.

KYRGYZSTAN

Stray from the typical teaching curriculum and land on the roof of the world— Central Asia remains virtually untouched by the tourism boom. Kyrgyzstan is the easiest country in Central Asia to enter with a Western passport, has a young capital (Bishkek), and is rich in nomadic culture. Though the city doesn't have much to offer by way of history, it has a bright nightlife and enough bars to pump you full of all the antifreeze you'll need to get through a Kyrgyz winter. Nearly entirely blanketed by the mighty Tian Shan mountain

range, the country offers some awesome trekking, horseback riding, and camping adventures. The Kyrgyz are known for their hospitality, but be prepared: they also have a strange penchant for Chinese food and karaoke. The London School in Bishkek (TheLondonSchool.org) offers TEFL jobs. As a foreign teacher, you'll get free accommodations and be paid fortnightly (a little foreign-speak for you).

TURKEY

In the interest of being upfront, you're not going to make megabucks here. But the country's ancient heritage and mix of international influence cast a spell on Westerners. We're talkin' ridiculous architecture, delicious grub, and gorgeous people. The Turkish middle class is eager to speak our language, and there are plenty of TEFL/ESL opportunities. Istanbul is pricey, so scoping out gigs in smaller cities is your best bet. No matter where you go, you'll be in the land of Turkish baths and the geographical wonders of Cappadocia and Ölüdeniz. For job postings, keep an eye on *Turkey Daily News* and Craigslist Istanbul. Try your luck with the English Centre, a language institute in Istanbul and online resources such as MyMerhaba (MyMerhaba.com).

NANNIES, MANNIES, AND MARY POPPINS: HOW TO WORK AS AN AU PAIR ABROAD

If you love watching *Blue's Clues* in a foreign language and chillin' with pint-size poopers, you might want to get into the au pair game. You can easily learn the basics of a language from a toddler, have a roof over your head, go places with the family that you'd never be able to afford to see on your own, and earn party money for your days off.

Europe and Singapore are popular destinations and the British Jobs Abroad Bulletin is your go-to site. Great Au Pair (Greatau pair.com) has listings for au pairs, babysitters, pet sitters, house sitters, senior caretakers, and tutors. This is not a job for nomads, but if you're planning on settling down for a while, you can make mad money watching rugrats.

If your only baby experience is playing peek-a-boo with your cousin's kid at Thanksgiving, forget about it. Blubbery minihumans expel shit (and other foul goo) that's not worth the time unless you're an experienced, cheek-pinching baby enthusiast.

WHERE TO PAIR?

Some countries (like Belgium) have strict regulations on non-EU au pairs. Italians tend to take their au pairs on summer

vacation and pay a little more for their services. Germans and the French prefer longer-term au pairs (six to twelve months) and require basic language skills in the host language. Native English-speaking au pairs are in high demand in Spain, and it's one of the best bets for easy job placement.

CREDS

If you want to stand out in a sea of nanny wannabes, make sure you've logged some hours babysitting at home with a formal agency that can write you a reference. Some countries and agencies require 200 hours of sitting before they'll consider taking you onboard. Brush up on your skills in the language of the country of your choice so you can at least babble with the babies (and understand your hosts!). Ditch your smoking habit while you're at it— while you might end up in a smoking household, you're more appealing to potential employers if you can check the nonsmoker box. First Aid certification is essential.

MANNIES

These days, mannies (or male nannies) are all the rage with the enlightened set. While there's still some hesitation in many places on letting the guys in on the kid fun, more agencies these days are accepting male applicants, particularly ones that place au pairs in France. And chicks dig dudes who are awesome with kids.

PLAYING GAMES, CHANGING LIVES

Your glory days of high school speedball domination may be long gone, but playing (and owning at) sports will forever live on. For all you gym-class-heroes-turned-vagabond-super tramps, volunteer organizations worldwide offer opportunities to live in foreign lands, play games, and change the lives of poverty-stricken kids on a daily basis.

KABUL, AFGHANISTAN

During Osama bin Laden's cave-hiding days, Kabul got bombed and shredded to pieces as part of the search. Today, Afghanistan's largest city is still recovering, and the youth of the nation are often forgotten amid all the chaos. Rather than waiting for the next bomb to drop, a group of international skaters got together and started Skateistan (Skateistan.org), a skateboarding school in Kabul where displaced local kids not only learn to skate, but also get instruction in language, arts, and civic responsibility. Kick-flip your volunteer career into action with Skateistan, where you can volunteer from your home country by organizing fund raising programs. Keep an eye out for the odd job available with the organization directly.

TRANSYLVANIA, ROMANIA

It's true that Transylvania is decorated with creepy castles, but it also packs hiking-friendly mountains and beachside resorts. Romania has been free from Communism since 1989, but this now-capitalist country could still use your help. Physical education is brushed aside throughout schooling, so more and more volunteer organizations are popping up to fill the gap. Your work-week will be split up between teaching and playing whichever sports you'd like at various orphanages, centers for disabled children, and day care centers for economically disadvantaged children—all of which seek out able-bodied and fun-spirited volunteers regularly.

ACCRA, GHANA

Formerly known as the Gold Coast and famous for its friendly inhabitants, the English-speaking country of Ghana is situated on Africa's west coast. Politically stable and safe, Ghana is one of the best places in which to experience your first African adventure; it's filled with beaches, offers safari tours, and boasts dense rain forests. The gold and cocoa plantations were once profitable enough to build a kingdom for the Ashanti (Ghana's largest tribe), but the country as a whole is terribly poor. Still, in 2006, Ghana kicked some serious ass in the World Cup, and the popularity of soccer in the country has since surged. Through the after-school sports coaching programs of Projects Abroad (Projects-abroad.com), you can spend two weeks of your summer (or a full year if you wish) as a soccer coach or camp counselor, helping enthusiastic kids reach their superstar potentials. A love of basketball is also creeping into the country, and similar opportunities are available.

RIGHTS

The sad truth about the world is that not everyone is granted even basic human rights. In many countries, social class, race, and gender play a large factor in the uneven distribution of rights. Whether your interest lies in helping women find freedom from sexual oppression or narrowing the gaps between social classes by volunteering in education, many international organizations exist to help you fight the good fight, all while further fueling your travels.

ALL ABOUT THE PEACE CORPS

The Peace Corps was created in 1961 to promote world peace and friendship by offering the helping hands of Americans to countries in need. Hundreds of thousands of volunteers have since served in over a hundred different countries.

Since the organization is so well established—and pretty selective—being a Peace Corps volunteer has become a rite of passage and an excellent résumé builder for anyone interested in a career in global development. A two-year stint in a foreign country with travel, food, and living expenses all taken care of does sound pretty sweet. But it isn't all peaceful handholding and love hugs. We'll shake down everything about this government-run program so you can better see if you want to climb up the Peace Corps tree.

THE MISSION

The agency asks for twenty-seven months of your time: three for in-country training on language, cross-cultural, technical, and health skills, and the remaining twenty-four for spending in an appointed host country fulfilling your duties. In return, they'll pay for your travel to and from the country, cover medical and dental expenses during service, provide you with living quarters, and give you a monthly allowance large enough to cover food. On top of that, you get a nice chunk of change (currently $8,000 before taxes) when your service is complete. As a Peace Corps volunteer, you can try your helpful hand at educating the world's youth; creating shelters, jobs, and opportunities; and keeping the planet green.

APPLICATION PROCESS

There are six separate fields in the program, all emphasizing education. You can apply for specific positions in Education; Health and HIV/AIDS; Business and Information and Communication Technology; Environment, Youth, and Community Development; and Agriculture. As long as you're an of-age US citizen you can apply, but since getting accepted has become fairly competitive, at least some background (college degree, prior experience, etc.) in a designated field will make you a much more appealing candidate. Jobs cycle fast, and the application process takes months, so get on it quick if you're game.

SOMETHING TO CONSIDER

In theory, the Peace Corps is a fantastic agency set out to better the world. In practice, many people have found their service to be a bit sketchy at times. Not all communities welcome wide-eyed Americans with open arms, and many have their own preconceived notions about our culture (or lack thereof). Manage your expectations, and—like you always should when traveling—stay alert. Many places that need help from the Peace Corps need it for a reason. They can be dangerous, unstructured, lawless lands, and, as a Peace Corps Volunteer (PVC), it's up to you to stay tight on your shit. Volunteers have

had their gear stolen, gotten sick through-out their service, fought with locals who sometimes aren't as friendly as you'd imag-ine, and—the Peace Corps' largest looming problem—have even been raped. Worst of all, among these unforseeable issues, is that the Peace Corps itself can be unre-sponsive and unhelpful. Try to envsion twenty-seven months of service before you sign up, 'cause it'll be a long time until you'll be back home dreaming about traveling again.

The Peace Corps definitely has its ups and downs. It won't exactly be fun or easy, but the best experiences never are. Some days will be long and grueling; others will be positively life changing—for you and those in your community.

THE HAPS WITH HABITAT

Habitat for Humanity is a Christian organization that's been at the forefront of building housing for those in need since the mid-'70s. Initially, Habitat aimed to build affordable housing for low-income Americans through the use of donated funds and labor. In 1984, former president Jimmy Carter participated in a building program in New York City that gave the organization a PR boost and caused Habitat's popularity to skyrocket. With the help of volunteers, they have built over half a million homes worldwide. You don't have to believe in Noah and his ark to volunteer your biceps' strength and hammering skills. Interna-tional programs run from six months to a year and are available in countries all over the world.

SEX SELLS SLAVES

All tassels aren't created equal. There are currently nearly thirty million slaves in the modern "free" world—more than at any other time in history. Thriving off of the reality that "sex sells," human trafficking is a severe, global atrocity that still goes largely unnoticed, despite the fact that it often takes place in plain view. Fortunately, there are many ways to be part of the solution, beginning with learning about the situation.

The human sex trade is a $32-billion-dollar-per-year business. Simply stated, slavery continues to exist because of greed and poverty. Sex is a profitable market, second only to illegal drugs, with many "business-men" dipping into both sex and drugs to double the financial gain. Like any sharp businessmen, human traffickers gauge their industry and pounce on opportunity. Wherever there is an extreme tragedy forcing victims into homelessness or desperation, there are lurking predators waiting in the wings to offer "assistance." Promising the poor and hungry a chance to eat and make money, these scumbag traffickers lure downtrodden women and men into working in brothels, massage parlors, and strip clubs, or onto the streets, where they work off their "debts." Most of the victims are women under the age of eighteen. Many are children handed over by their own parents, who are tricked into believing that they are sending their kid to learn a legitimate trade that will eventually bring money into the household. Human trafficking is prevalent wherever there is poverty, but especially throughout Southeast Asia, Africa, India, Eastern Europe, and South America.

GIVING WOMEN REAL CHOICES

Numerous organizations are attempting to abolish modern slavery by empowering victims to financially sustain themselves and their families and providing them

alternatives to selling their bodies to survive. Various organizations are working toward a solution by providing a space for women to sell their handmade items and showcase their other skills. Global Mamas (Global Mamas.org) empowers African women from various regions by creating a global marketplace around their handmade goods like traditional batik fabrics, glass beads, shea butter, and recycled plastic accessories. Other organizations like Not For Sale are partnering with sister groups around the globe to set up job-training programs for human-trafficking victims. These programs also offer safe shelter, holistic healing classes, and day care to help victims transition.

WAYS YOU CAN HELP

It is important to remember that, without demand, there is no need for supply. We're not suggesting that you never go to a strip club again, but disengaging yourself from the activities that perpetuate the problem will lessen the demand. Sex tourism in places like Thailand encourages people to travel to certain destinations solely for the opportunity to meet underage girls and boys. If something seems creepy, it probably is—hands off! There are hundreds of ways to get involved in the movement to end modern slavery. If you fancy yourself a writer or designer, contact one of the many organizations like Not For Sale and donate your talent and time. Next time you have a gift to buy in countries where sex trafficking is prevalent, seek out items handmade by women and make purchases with a purpose.

NAKED AWARENESS
Prostitution and stripping are not always tied to modern slavery. People often make an educated, empowered choice to participate in these professions, and there's nothing wrong with that. But for those whose "choice" is a life-or-death situation, their bodies and lives are no longer their own. As backpackers who love a good, sexy time, we need to be aware of this dehumanizing atrocity and start becoming part of the solution. No effort is too small—except no effort at all.

WILL WORK FOR FOOD

While everyone's interpretation of what makes a good meal varies culturally, one thing is universal across the board: we all need to eat. The problem is, over a billion people around the world don't (and can't), due to factors like lack of access to adequate food sources, droughts, natural disasters, or civil conflicts. The benefits of dropping off a bowl of rice and beans (an approach taken by some relief organizations) are short-lived, and volunteer programs are often too temporary to make a real difference. Building your career around alleviating world hunger—now that's a tasty idea that sits well in the stomach.

GET YOUR CREDS
Devoting your life to combating hunger starts with getting a degree in the field. The main umbrella for this sort of work is known as International Development, and you can study the field at all levels (BA, MA, and PhD). If you want to get more specific, there are programs that go into the economics of food scarcity and security, agricultural development, nutrition, and logistics (moving food from developed to developing countries), among others.

START SMALL
If you like getting down and dirty, there are plenty of opportunities to work directly with local communities on a smaller scale. If you want to be outdoors, check into small sustainable farms that need help with planting, reaping seasonal harvests, and transporting food to markets. Working at food banks (both at home and abroad) will usually put you in direct contact with those who need a helping hand. If you're obsessed with food documentaries and read books like *The Omnivore's Dilemma*, put all of that food knowledge to use and teach nutrition classes in communities that have high rates of malnutrition. If Fair Trade is your game, find organizations that advocate for fair wages paid to small farmers in exchange for their quality produce.

FUCK IT, GO BIG!

An industry giant, the United Nations' World Food Programme (WFP) is first to respond when disasters strike and wipe out food sources. These guys also work to prepare for emergencies before they happen, as well as educate communities worldwide on nutrition and agriculture. Another huge NGO that dominates the field is the Food and Agriculture Organization (FAO) of the United Nations. The FAO focuses on everything from sustainable farming practices to researching water scarcities. Both organizations are constantly looking for internationally-minded individuals with varied skills, and offer opportunities that place employees and interns on projects all around the world. Pick up some creds working in the field and apply to the opportunities these big shots have available.

FIVE BEST COUNTRIES TO STUDY ABROAD FOR POLITICAL SCIENCE MAJORS

If you're studying to be one of our country's political greats, gaining a worldly perspective puts politics into a broader context. Once you've sorted your Washingtons and Hamiltons stateside, check out a political science program abroad to add international knowledge to your think bank. Take advantage of our local study break suggestions but keep in mind that it's easy for people to blackmail you with foreign debauchery when you run for governor.

EUROPE: GENEVA, SWITZERLAND

The global fondue melting pot of Geneva is one of the world's most important cities financially and diplomatically. It's home to the second-biggest United Nations office (after New York City) and many other intergovernmental agencies. Most poli-sci study abroad programs here focus on international relations (you know, because of the whole Geneva Convention thing?). Known as the "Capital of Peace," the Swiss capital's army is equipped with tweezers, a toothpick, nail file, and corkscrew that all fold away into a nice red pocket knife. You'll be safe.

Study Break!

Situated between two lakes and surrounded by dominating mountain ranges, Interlaken is the adventure sports capital of Europe. Whether you want to skydive, bungee jump, go canyoning (see page 26), hang glide, or scale a glacier, this is the spot for good, old-fashioned shit-your-pants adventure.

AUSTRALIA:
CANBERRA, AUSTRALIA

One hundred years ago, presumably over a Fosters, an old convict from Sydney met with an old convict from Melbourne and pitted each respective colony's best boxing kangaroos against each other in a death match that would determine which city would be Australia's capital. When the match ended in a draw, a random location between the cities was chosen, and Canberra became the capital. Here, you can learn more about this and other fascinating Australian law-making processes in the Parliamentary Internship Program—a program that lets you work directly with members of Australia's Parliament for a full semester of college credit.

Study Break!

Fraser Island in Queensland is the world's largest sand island. College students flock to party here with water so turquoise it looks Photoshopped and sand so powdery white it would excite, confuse, and ultimately disappoint Scarface.

AFRICA:
GABARONE, BOTSWANA

Botswana has a stable, well-run government in a continent where corrupt governments are as plentiful as blood diamonds. You'll study the politics of Botswana as well as Africa's role in world politics at a top African university.

Study Break!

The massive Okavango Delta attracts a dense concentration of Africa's big mammals with its expansive crystal clear water channels. You can row around in dugout canoes and camp in the open among wildlife with no fences or cages. It's like a weekend camping trip to your local state park—if your local state park had elephants, hippos, lions, hyenas, rhinos, and zebras roaming freely.

SOUTH AMERICA:
SANTIAGO, CHILE

The capital of one of the fastest growing economies in South America, Chile is home to a trio of universities with world-class political science programs and was rated the second-best city for students in Latin America. All courses are held in Spanish, so you'll get plenty of practice in the language with the most native speakers in the world outside of Chinese.

Study Break!

Head way south to Torres del Paine National Park in southern Patagonia. On the four-day trek you'll see jagged snow capped peaks, avalanches crumbling down mountainsides, icebergs calving off glaciers, and the iconic granite towers. The entire trek is near sea level, so there's no threat of altitude sickness.

ASIA:
HONG KONG

As East Asia lines itself up to be the center of the global economy, Hong Kong offers a unique perspective with its combination of Western and Eastern influences. You can get a study abroad two-fer as many poli-sci programs here emphasize bilingualism and biculturalism.

Study Break!

Take a ferry across to Macau, Asia's Las Vegas. Make a few short-term investments at a casino, and then blow your winnings at a club. Remember to save a bit for the Macau Tower bungee jump—the highest in the world at over 760 feet.

SUSTAIN-ABILITY

It's no secret that our world is in crisis ecologically. While sorting your recycling and refusing plastic bags is a good start, if you're passionate about sustainability, your time can be better spent digging your hands into environmental issues abroad. Working on sustainability projects, in many cases, will be a chance to escape the big cities and learn about the local culture from the ground up. By picking your own dinner on an organic farm or helping to build a school out of upcycled plastic bottles, you'll be helping sustain the planet for generations of backpackers to come.

ODD JOBS TO FUND YOUR TRAVELS

Freedom isn't free. Leaving The Man behind may have been the reason for your trip, but he's still out there—lurking in every corner of the world—demanding that you pay up. With work visas and employment restrictions, you can't simply slap on a suit and tie and sell your soul for a little dough on the road. But don't worry. There are plenty of ways to boost that bank account while you're livin' the life—and none of them require paperwork or government approval.

Get Crafty

Making cool shit and selling it on the street is the most popular way backpackers keep the cash flow positive. The possibilities are endless, and you don't need much capital to get started. You can eat for weeks by making necklaces and earrings from shells, discarded wire, and pretty river stones. Stock up on string and hooks in a big city. But be warned: in certain countries or cities it might be illegal or even require a permit to sell products or collect shells, so be sure to do your research first!

Go Green

European festivals are breeding grounds for cold, hard cash. In many countries, like Germany, you can trade in plastic bottles for moolah. Most festival-goers are too stoned to worry about where they leave their recycling; consequently, surrounding campgrounds become treasure troves of plastic bottles waiting to be traded for cash.

Tried and True

Offering your own sweat and blood is the oldest trick in the book, and it works like a charm. Hostels often need an extra pair of hands in the kitchen or bar and will offer you a free bed and/or cheap food in exchange. It's a prime gig for meeting people—who doesn't want to cozy up to the bartender?

Get Techy

Turn your sporadically updated travel blog into cold hard cash. Sound like some Silicon Valley daydreaming bullshit? Well, it isn't. You've surely seen stories of people leaving everything behind and taking to the road for years at a time while only making money blogging. How? You have to put creative thought into it, take kick-ass pictures, and build up a social following. Think of it as less of a hobby and more of a part-time job. There is a market for vicarious travel and if you're providing that service for enough people, advertising and sponsored content will arise.

Kick It and Flip It

If circumventing the globe is in your travel plan, with a little forethought, this gig makes fiscal sense. While chilling in cheaper countries, like India or Thailand, stock up on cool, lightweight hippie shit. When you make it to the other side of the world, sell it at street fairs or festivals.

WWOOF, WWOOF, BABY!

We're not talking about barking. WWOOFing stands for "World Wide Opportunities on Organic Farms"-ing. This network (WWOOF) was developed to link volunteers to organic farms with available volunteer opportunities. You volunteer on an international farm for an agreed amount of hours, and they feed and house your hungry, broke ass. Pretty fair deal. Nothing extravagant here, but given the prices of organic, fresh-from-the-ground food and housing, it's a good trade-off.

THE PRODUCTION PROBLEM

Unfortunately, the factory farming method of meat production in the United States is spreading its long arm overseas. By now, you have all seen the hidden camera videos of animals on large farms being abused and neglected, and of chickens with breasts so large that their legs break cramped in tiny spaces to maximize production. Our cows are diseased, pigs are electrocuted, and turkeys are strangled, and all in the name of producing the millions of burgers, nuggets, and who-the-fuck-knows-whats we're all so attached to.

When animals become commodities and farms are replaced by factories, raising and slaughtering animals becomes a quest to turn higher profits with no concern for comfort. In response, some have chosen to become vegetarians, while others have deferred their hard-earned cash to more expensive organic, free-range meat and dairy options. Being a vegetarian, vegan, or organic/free-range meat-eater is a statement; rolling up your sleeves and actually getting down and dirty at a farm is putting your statement into action.

Y'ALL CITY FOLK? NO PROBLEM

No farming experience is necessary to WWOOF with the best of them. Daily duties range from milking cows to plowing, sowing, maintaining animal sheds, and planting seeds. This work will be hard, and you will get that ugly farmer's tan, but your contribution will be greatly appreciated and rewarded.

By volunteering, you get to live in a foreign country of your choice as a farmer (which is the closest you can get to local culture) and escape the tourist traps by living in the countryside. Plus, you get the freshest food available in the region, daily.

HOW TO START LIVING OFF THE LAND

Whether you're a vegetarian looking to support small farms or a meat-eater looking for a unique (and damn cheap) way to live and eat abroad, hooking up with a farm through the WWOOF network is a good idea. While your friends back home are eating canned, frozen, and pesticide-covered produce, you'll be holding a fresh, organic vegetable in one hand and a hoe in the other.

→ WWOOFing organizations exist almost everywhere in the world where there is a farm. There is no global membership, but you sometimes have to pay a small, country-specific annual fee (used to maintain the organization) to join the WWOOFing network. For instance, the annual fee in Argentina costs $38, but in Guatemala it's only $4. Go to WWOOF. net, pick a country, pay your fee, and you'll get a list of farms.

- Choose your ideal farm (animal, fruit and vegetable, grain, or a combination) from the list. Keep in mind the type of work will correlate with the kind of farm you choose. So, if squeezing udders makes you shudder, stick to produce production.
- Contact the farm to make a volunteer arrangement. Find out about: duration of the volunteer opportunity, hours of work per day, days of work per week, type of accommodations offered (tent, private/shared room), and proximity of surrounding towns.
- Get a plane ticket, put on some sunscreen, and get to work.

BOTTLE SCHOOLS

Hug It Forward, a United States–based nonprofit, takes the "Reduce, Reuse, Recycle" mantra to a new level. In 2009, these guys began constructing "bottle schools" from plastic bottles and other trash in Guatemala. Most of the villages where bottle schools are built are rural and poor, often hours from a paved road. These trashy classrooms are often the first schools the villages have ever had. Since they started playing with trash, Hug It Forward has erected more than seventy schools and counting.

BOTTLE AND MORTAR

The first step to building a bottle school is to collect thousands of plastic bottles and make them into ecobricks by stuffing them full of inorganic trash (to prevent the school from rotting). The frame is built from concrete and iron for strength. Then, the ecobricks are stacked on top of each other and sandwiched between chicken wire. A couple layers of cement are slapped on for good measure, and then the building gets its Central American mojo when it's painted in festive colors.

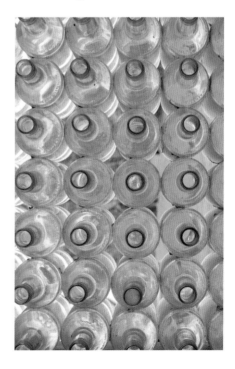

These schools aren't built in a day, or without plenty of lending hands. Serve the World Today, a for-profit company, runs voluntourism trips in coordination with Hug It Forward. By volunteering your time and taking a trip down, you can do some good for Guatemala.

PLASTIC WITH A PURPOSE

A bottle school is an in-yo-face testimonial to the possibility of local building, even in the most remote or impoverished communities. But there's more than radical ecoconstruction going on here—building a bottle school cleans a community's bottle-clogged gutters, educates local kids about recycling, and, in the end, gives kids a space within which to learn and play.

PROGRAM PERKS

A bottle school trip includes a coffee farm tour, cultural talks, meals prepared by a private cook, and trips to the trippy Mayan ruins at Mixco Viejo and the city of Antigua, a UNESCO World Heritage site. Most important, because you'll be working shoulder-to-shoulder with the locals, you'll have the chance to build relationships with both Guatemalans and other volunteers.

A bottle school trip costs around $1,299, which covers everything but your transportation to Guatemala, booze, and souvenirs. Additionally, every bottle school volunteer is asked to fund-raise $250 for the project predeparture. However you decide to do this is up to you, but Hug It Forward (HugItForward.net) has some fun suggestions, and every cent of the money you raise goes directly to a school project. Just like every small piece of trash that eventually constructs a school, every penny counts.

HOW TO BIKE AROUND EUROPE

Riding a bike through Europe is a unique and interesting way to explore as it allows you to gain access to roads not navigable by larger vehicles. It's also easy on the pockets, saving you hundreds of dollars in transportation costs, and the environment won't hate you as a result. So get off your ass (then back on it) and pump your pedals 'till you puke.

Bike Sharing

You do not need to own a bike to ride in Europe. While the US finally figured out bike sharing and has rolled out programs like NYC's Citi Bike and Boston's Hubway, Europe has been tinkering with bike sharing for years, putting in lots of trial and error (i.e., mostly getting people to stop stealing bikes and dishonoring the honor system). Throughout many parts of Europe, most notably the Netherlands and France, bike sharing works quite similarly to a library card. Basically, you create a membership with a company, such as Vélib' in Paris, and you pick up a bike at their station, use it, then drop it at any other station (they have tons all over the city). Variations of this system can be found in Germany (Call a Bike), Amsterdam (OV-fiets) and many other places in Europe. Bike sharing is cheap, fun, earth-friendly and gives you a reason to wear spandex (because with no reason, spandex is unjustifiable).

European Bike Express

For a different take on biking Europe, catch a ride on the European Bike Express, a coach line offering comfortable transportation for you and your bike. EBE stops in over thirty cities in Europe, opening up the UK, France, Northern Spain, Germany and Switzerland to your two-wheelin' pursuits. The bus offers entertainment, comfortable reclining chairs, and plenty of like-minded travelers to shoot the cycling shit with.

Since your drop-off and pick-up locations don't have to match, you can experience a variety of cultures and sites in one trip.

Gastrobiking

Biking around Europe will make you hungry. Eating around Europe will require you to exercise. The French combined the two to solve this food and cycling dilemma. It's called gastrobiking and it offers the best of both worlds with food and cycling tours through Southeastern France. Gastrobiking offers tours full of long climbs, sweeping descents, delicious pastries, fine wines, fantastic meals, quaint cafés, and quiet roads. The tours range from weekend trips to cyclosportives–or long distance, organized cycling events.

STUDY BY SUNLIGHT

Energy doesn't always have to come from a power line. The almighty sun shoots out its rays free of charge and is strong enough to power the world on its own. Since lighting up classrooms uses tons of electricity, certain colleges are playing a part in building a better environment by looking to the sun for assistance. Green-light your study abroad semester with one of these ecoconscious colleges.

ARCADIA UNIVERSITY: BONN, GERMANY

Arcadia's program in Bonn is the perfect place to study solar power. Germany is a leader in renewable energy and this five-week summer study course shines a light on the policies and development of renewable energy while offering first-hand trips to see what the university and surrounding cities are doing to utilize solar power. Check out nearby Paris, Amsterdam, and Brussels on your own weekend excursions while crossing off environmental science or language requirements during the week.

UNIVERSITY OF LAUSANNE: SWITZERLAND

Like Germany, Switzerland is one of the world's pioneers and leaders in sustaining and recycling energy. The University of Lausanne offers plenty of study abroad options spanning shortened semesters to the full academic year. Lausanne (both the city and University) is a world-renowned innovator in solar energy research and you can lock down a degree in Energy Management and Sustainability while studying in state-of-the-art facilities.

CARDIFF UNIVERSITY: WALES

Cardiff is one of Britain's leading research institutions. Its study abroad programs prompt you to take two required courses and two electives over the semester and will fit nicely in completing credentials for engineering, mathematics, or science majors. You'll learn about solar and other forms of renewable energy in your course on recyclable energy research and implementation. Even better, you'll dive deep into Welsh life by living, breathing, and studying the capital's literature, language, and culture.

GREEN: ICELAND

The coolest (but not coldest) spot in the northernmost part of the world, Iceland is more than just a giant geothermal tub of sexiness (although, there's that too). GREEN (Global Renewable Energy Education Network) is an exclusive, educational program that teaches renewable energy and sustainability through adventure excursions and exposure to Nordic culture. Programs in Iceland are short (eight to ten days) and are offered during summer, winter, and spring breaks. Your studies will start out in the classroom but will quickly turn into group adventures outdoors. As short and rewarding as it is, GREEN will give you up to 1.5 college credits when you transfer the program back to your university.

ONLY YOU CAN PREVENT FOREST FIRES

Becoming a park ranger is no easy task. But if your love of the outdoors and keeping it pristine is matched only by your passion for helping others respect the green, start learning your plants and animals and branch out internationally. Rubbing elbows with Smokey the Bear outside the US will take some preparation and hard work, but the payoff can be well worth the effort. Bonus: You get to be a legit lumbersexual without getting shit for it.

BEFORE YOU APPLY

For the extreme outdoor enthusiast, being a park ranger might seem like its all unicorns-and-cupcakes, but in reality, the job can be more about shoveling bear shit and fighting with drunken assholes who insist that burning plastic is hilarious. Keep in mind that if you want to get to a point where you can get paid (very little) to play outside, you will first have to clock in some work hours. Overall, no matter which country you want to park it in, plan on studying something relevant like park management, zoology, or botany before or during your stay. You may also have to volunteer to get your foot in the (out)doors.

PLAYING IN AUSSIE PARKS

Park Victoria is responsible for managing hundreds of killer national, state, and metropolitan parks as well as thousands of conservation reserves in Victoria, Australia. Noncitizens can only become park rangers in the land down under if they have a valid working visa. Plan on hitting the books hard in Natural Resource Management and Recreation/Tourism to be considered. The Summer Ranger Program offers a limited number of short-term ranger jobs for students and is a great "in" to the Aussie park system.

AFRICAN RANGE

If you feel like parks are just crappy slides and picnics, you might want to consider heading to Africa to become a badass safari ranger. Learn how to track wild animals and survive in the bush while dodging the bullets of poachers. Outside of the zoology courses and personal training sessions you will want to complete beforehand, enroll in a Safari Ranger School to get thorough training about ranger life in the African wild. Those afraid of snakes, rhinos, or physical exertion need not apply.

OTP Tip: If you get really serious about ranger-ing (e.g., you've invested in pair of too-short khakis), join the Rangers without Borders (IRF) international rangers organization; it'll be useful when you've petted one rabid squirrel too many.

COLOMBIAN PARK CARE

Colombia has an array of parks scattered around the country. Some parks contain glaciers and beaches; others are more like full-on leafy forests. The scenery here should hit that nature g-spot for any aspiring ranger. To apply for the volunteer ranger program you'll need to present some basic documents like a passport and certification that you're healthy and not crazy, and get a couple of precautionary vaccines and photos. The program runs a five-day training period, after which you will be assigned to your park of choice and given free lodging and in-park transportation. You'll have to pay for your meals, but if you study up, perhaps foraging something edible will be in the cards.

WRAPPING UP

We hope this book has made you uncomfortably anxious to travel and helped you realize that the material things holding you back are worthless. By no means is this text exhaustive; it is simply a glimpse into the wonderful underworld of travel, filled with street food, art, music, parties, and the opportunity to learn about the world through real expreiences.

On the road, you'll learn that travel is only partially about the destination. Being out of your element—wherever you are in the world—teaches you to tap into your survival skills physically, mentally, and socially. You will figure out valuable lessons about yourself and how you respond to crazy new situations. Some people you meet will lead lives wildly different from yours, and others will be eerily similar. You will find that friendship is universal; that language barriers are easy to overcome; that no matter how broke you are, there is always a way to get a drink, share a laugh, and dance like you mean business. You will sleep standing up, eat lying down, sprint through airports and bus stations like an Olympic athlete, get thrown off your intended path only to find something much more exciting, discuss political theory using mostly hand gestures and grunts, and love every minute of it.

When browsing through other people's travel photos just won't cut it anymore, we urge you to start planning a trip of your own. Before you get bogged down with student loans, mortgages, kids, spouses, and responsibilities, learn a little about yourself by hitting the road. You don't need much money to have the time of your life abroad, as long as you decide that comfort can wait, that food tastes better street-side, and that being a little grimy isn't a big deal. Sacrifice to disappear, and the world becomes yours.

THE AUTHORS

ANNA STAROSTINETSKAYA

Anna was born in Ukraine, raised in Los Angeles, spent a New York minute in Brooklyn, and currently resides in San Francisco, California. Her most memorable trip was to Spain, where she hopped a fence on the side of a highway to sample an authentic Spanish olive right from a tree. Don't eat olives from trees for two reasons: (1) they have not been cured and taste like utter shit, and (2) if the grove's owner catches you trespassing, you may leave Spain with more battle wounds than you intended.

BRIAN BIROS

A veteran on the backpacker circuit, Brian has circled the globe thrice, leaving a sticky trail across eighty-plus countries. Originally from Chicago, he's lived all over the US and parts of South America, most recently giving his backpack a rest in San Francisco. But these days, you're more likely to find him partying in a Budapest hostel bar, sipping tea on a Himalayan mountain trek, dogging downward in a Nicaraguan beach yoga class, or dancing into the sunrise at Burning Man. If you see him, tell him to call home.

CHRISTOPHER PLATIS

One of OTP's first writers and editors, Chris recently spent some time bruising his tidbits in Switzerland and schmoozing his way into Berlin's clubs and art scene. When he's not writing, he's either out testing his travel gear, exploring coasts and corners in pursuit of the perfect beach,

or tracing his roots back in Greece, where he operates a boutique hotel.

LISETTE CHERESSON

Skipping the seas and spreading her word seed, Lisette was OTP's first senior editor and a New York–based writer, filmmaker, and adventuress. She's currently the Managing Editor at Wanderlust where her love for green living, yoga, and words intersect. Lisette has been to more than thirty countries—if you're looking to feed monkeys in South America, trek through monastery towns in Burma, guerilla camp in Cambodia, or get naked on the Great Wall of China, she's your go-to gal for advice.

SARA M. WHITE

A little sweet, a little sour, and a whole lotta spicy, Sara is a quirky ball of travel-writing genius. She spent some time studying theater and dance in Bali, taught English in Thailand, and called Brooklyn home for many years before switching coasts to get her MFA in screenwriting at UCLA. While most people would love to brag about just riding an elephant, not only did this girl mount the beast for a gallop, but she also bathed it for extra credit. She's an overachiever; we like that.

SARAH BINION

Sarah is happiest sitting on a train reading Paul Theroux and double fisting wine and coffee. Her favorite journey by rail was aboard the Dacia Express between Bucharest and Vienna (she even named her dog Dacia after the experience). When she's not dousing her self in beverages aboard the world's finest trains you can find her among the vineyards in Eastern Europe, Sonoma, and South America working with her partners and small holder grape farmers living in poverty to create sexy wines for the socially conscious.

CREATIVE DIRECTOR: FREDDIE PIKOVSKY

The ringmaster of OTP, Freddie fell in love with backpacking on a trip throughout Europe in 2009 that ended in travel enlightenment. Soon after he moved to a Brooklyn hostel and lived among broke-ass travelers for nearly a year, ultimately inspiring the creation of OTP. Freddie has since explored the world, from South America to Iceland, South East Asia, and across the US. He is passionate to inspire every young person to experience the life-changing capabilities of travel and drives OTP to make this vision a reality.

Special thanks to:

Adil Dara Kim
Bianca Rappaport
Connie Nguyen
Erin Ridley
Jaclyn Einis
Kyle McNichols
Lorenzo R. Ramos
Mark Ayling
Taveeshi Singh
Timothy Melough

This book would not have been possible without the people who have supported our mission throughout our journey. Thank you to all of you who have contributed your talents, advice, and good vibes along the way.

PHOTO CREDITS

6: Freddie Pikovsky; p. 8: Barnacles Hostels; p. 9: The Adventurists; p. 10 (top left): Freddie Pikovsky; p. 10 (top right) and end papers: Luca Boldrini; p. 10 (middle) and end papers: Graham "gtall1"; p. 10 (bottom left): Neil Simmons; p. 10 (bottom right): yolanda.white84; p. 12 (top): Freddie Pikovsky; p. 12 (middle left) and end papers: "darkday"; p. 12 (middle right): Freddie Pikovsky; p. 12 (bottom): Flying Kiwi Tours; p. 14 and end papers: J Brew "brewbooks"; p. 15: Siri Schwartzman; p. 16: Sascha Grabow, Saschagrabow.com; p. 17: Aviachar Avinash Achar; p. 19 (top left) and end papers: Mark Dumont; p. 19 (top right): Cl.udio Dias Timm; p. 19 (bottom left): Pardee Ave.; p. 19 (bottom middle): April Nobile; p. 19 (bottom right): Anna J. Phillips, Renzo Arauco-Brown, Alejandro Oceguera-Figeroa, Gloria P. Gomez, Maria Beltrán, Yi-Te Lai, Mark E. Siddall; p. 20: "pulaw"; p. 21 (top) and end papers: Hairi "hairibaba"; p. 21 (bottom): "Deortiz"; p. 23: Richard Giddins; p. 24 (top): BiblioArchives/LibraryArchives; p. 24 (bottom): Mack Male; p. 25: Andrew Purdam; p. 26 (left): Philip Larson; p. 26 (right): GaudiAZ; p. 27: GaudiAZ; p. 28: Rob Chandler; p. 29: Anthony Cramp; p. 31: NeilsPhotography, Neilsrtw.blogspot.com; p. 32: "karlnorling," Jno.se/; p. 33: JorgeBRAZIL; p. 34: Ipoh kia; p. 35 (top): Mark "Strength"; p. 35 (bottom): Andrew Bowden; p. 36: Duncan Brown (Cradlehall); p. 37 and end papers: Warren Rohner; p. 38: Chris Martin; p. 40: Carlos Andrés Reyes; p. 41: "chelsiefoty"; p. 42: "descubriendoelmundo"; p. 43: Luis Alejandro Bernal Romero; p. 44 (top): Douglas Scortegagna; p. 44 (bottom): "Dimitry B."; p. 45: "Dimitry B."; p. 46 (top left): Freddie Pikovsky; p. 46 (top right): "claumoho"; p. 46 (middle): Freddie Pikovsky; p. 46 (bottom left): Freddie Pikovsky; p. 46 (bottom right): "Dun.can"; p. 48: Dominique Darcy; p. 49 and end papers: "ifindkarma"; p. 51: Laura Padgett; p. 52 (left): Meindert van D; p. 52 (right): Radamantis Torres; p. 53 (top) and end papers: Alex Torrenegra; p. 53 (bottom): Rob Shenk; p. 55: Colin and Sarah Northway; p. 56: Carolyn Conner; p. 57 (top) and end papers: Ira Mowen; p. 57 (bottom): b.frahm; p. 58: Mark Fischer; p. 59 (top) and end papers: Mark Fischer; p. 59 (middle): Jean-François Gornet; p. 59 (bottom): Thomas Maluck; p. 60: "drnan tu"; p. 61: "verygreen"; p. 62: Sergey Norin; p. 63: Axel Axel "ikhou"; p. 64 (left): Peter Cigliano; p. 64 (right top) and end papers: Karen Green; p. 64 (right bottom): DJ Philly G; p. 65: Rob React; p. 66: Salim Virji; p. 67 (left): Moyan Brenn; p. 67 (right): Jean-Pierre Dalbéra; p. 68: Jean-Pierre Dalbéra; p. 69 and end papers: Freddie Pikovsky; p. 70 (top) and end papers: John McSporran; p. 70 (bottom): Freddie Pikovsky; p. 73: Jorge from Tokyo; p. 74 (top left) and end papers: Christopher Michel; p. 74 (top right): "Russ"; p. 74 (bottom left): Freddie Pikovsky; p. 74: (bottom right): "photonetworkgroup"; p. 75 (left): Susan Sermoneta; p. 75 (right): Howard Galicia; p. 76: นางสาว นฤมล สมบุญ; p. 77: Toby Oxborrow; p. 78: Simon Fraser University; p. 79 (left) and end papers: San Sharma; p. 79 (right): Simon Fraser University; p. 81: Thomas Edwards; p. 82 (left): Ricardo 清介 八木; p. 82 (right) and end papers: Ricardo 清介 八木; p. 83 (left): Catherine "rumpleteaser"; p. 83 (right top): "Otakumunidad Damned"; p. 83 (right bottom): Matias Tukiainen; p. 85 (left): "cute as heck"; p. 85 (right): David Berkowitz; p. 86: "Yenkassa"; p. 88 (top): The Global Panorama; p. 88 (middle left): Freddie Pikovsky; p. 88 (middle right): Freddie Pikovsky; p. 88 (bottom): Freddie Pikovsky; p. 89 and end papers: Derek Key; p. 90 (left): Phil Denton; p. 90 (right) and end papers: Paul Arps; p. 91: Paul Arps; p. 92 (left): stu_spivack; p. 92 (right): "spine186"; p. 94: TheGirlsNY – Kim; p. 95 and end papers: "Loozrboy"; p. 98: Icelandenquirer.blogspot.com; p. 99: "Lil Wolf"; p. 100: "Chris 73"; p. 103: Richard @ Ladyous.blogspot.com; p. 104: Visitingeu.com; p. 105: "chee.hong"; p. 106 and end papers: Sandra C

Qinn; p. 108: rugbyxm, Ryan Erickson; p. 109: Sara Goldsmith; p. 110 (left): "Kudo Momo"; p. 110 (right): Michael Voelker; p. 111 (top): Caryl Joan Estrosas; p. 111 (bottom): Joseph A Ferris III; p. 112 (top) and end papers: Alan Kleina Mendes; p. 112 (middle left): Jean-Pierre Dalbéra; p. 112 (middle right) and end papers: Christian Senger; p. 112 (bottom): Luke Addison; p. 113 (left): Gerardo Lazzari; p. 113 (right): Freddie Pikovsky; p. 114: Elizabeth Burnett; p. 115: Jamie Bellal; p. 118: Joe Lodge; p. 119: Clément Belleudy; p. 120: Chris "Effervescing"; p. 121 (top): Hunter Desportes; p. 121 (bottom): "Yo Pizza"; p. 124 (top): Eva Rinaldi; p. 124 (middle left): Cata "K 13"; p. 125 (middle right): Freddie Pikovsky; p. 124 (bottom): Marc Love; p. 127: Martin Fisch; p. 128 and end papers: Team at Carnaval.com Studios; p. 129 (left): Brazil Women's Beach Volleyball Team; p. 129 (right): Marek Krzystkiewicz; p. 131: Freddie Pikovsky; p. 132: Ben Askins; p. 133: Eric Huybrechts; p. 135: "Nickel Bag of Funk"; p. 136: Yun Huang Yong; p. 137: Rose of Academe; p. 140 (left): Greg - ssy; p. 140 (right) and end papers: Mazarias Antoranz; p. 141: Montserrat Labiaga Ferrer; p. 142 (top left): TheDoGoodDames; p. 142 (top right) and end papers: ITSpeaks, Wikimedia Commons; p. 142 (middle): Freddie Pikovsky; p. 142 (bottom left): Mike Photo Art; p. 142 (bottom right): Jeremy Brooks; p. 144: Kamilla Oliveira; p. 146: Peanut Dela Cruz; p. 147 and end papers: Jurgen "300tdorg"; p. 148 (top): Staff Sgt. Russell Lee Klika, US Army National Guard; p. 148 (bottom): Dominic Rivard; p. 151: MRGT, Margot Gabel; p. 152 (left) and end papers: Helder Ribeiro; p. 152 (right) and end papers: garryknight, Garry Knight; p. 154 (left): LollyKnit; p. 154 (right): Kate Ter Haar; p. 155: Okinawa Steve; p. 156 (top) and end papers: Ryan Maple; p. 156 (bottom left): Patrick Yodarus; p. 156 (bottom right): Ian Mackenzie; p. 159: J Aaron Farr; p. 160: Robert Couse-Baker; p. 162: Ramnath Bhat; p. 163: macgodbrad, "bclinesmith"; p. 164 (left) and end papers: Constanza.CH; p. 164 (right): Helder Ribeiro; p. 165 and end papers: Didier Baertschiger; p. 166: William Alphonsus Butler, Masterbutler.tumblr.com; p. 168: Joseph De Palma; p. 169: Rob Dammers; p. 171 and end papers: jbozanowski, Jakub Bozanowski; p. 176: Michael Mandiberg; p. 177: Charles Dyer; p. 178: jdklub, Justin Klubnik; p. 179: Matthias Ripp; p. 181: "cmor15"; p. 182 and end papers: Angelo De Mesa; p. 183: West Midlands Police; p. 185: Max-Leonhard von Schaper; p. 190: Raumrot.com; p. 192 (left): Joe Stump; p. 192 (right): Freddie Pikovsky; p. 194 and end papers: Matt Corks; p. 195: Holi Drunk@Mumbai, "hermesmerana"; p. 198 (top) and end papers: darlene is evil; p. 198 (middle left): Mathias Appel; p. 198 (middle right): Freddie Pikovsky; p. 198 (bottom): Daniel Thornton; p. 200: Freddie Pikovsky; p. 203 (top) and end papers: Liam Quinn; p. 203 (bottom): Nathan Johnson; p. 205: US Army Africa; p. 206: DFID – UK Department for International Development; p. 208: Nico Kaiser; p. 211: International Federation of Library Associations; p. 212 (left): Ton Rulkens; p. 212 (right): Augapfel, Christopher Billman; p. 213 (left): Peter Broster; p. 213 (right) and end papers: Ellen Forsyth; p. 214 (left): Children's Organization of Southeast Asia; p. 214 (right): ResoluteSupportMedia; p. 216: "zapstratosphere"; p. 217: Peter Gene; p. 218: Nadya Peek; p. 219: nova3web – Oluniyi Ajao; p. 220: US Mission Canada; p. 221: National Museum of American History; p. 222: KOMUnews; p. 223: Ira Gelb; p. 225 (left): Giro555SHO, Samenwerkende Hulporganisaties; p. 225 (right): RON SOMBILON MEDIA, ART AND PHOTOGRAPHY; p. 226 and end papers: Freddie Pikovsky; p. 228: "blaizepascall"; p. 231: Kris Carillo; p. 232: nist6ss, Twentyfour Students; p. 236 (top): Freddie Pikovsky; p. 236 (middle left): José Antonio Morcillo Valenciano; p. 236 (middle right): Umesh Bansal; p. 236 (bottom) and end papers: Freddie Pikovsky; p. 237: "russellstreet"

INDEX